JOHNNY DEPP
BIOGRAPHY

A LIFE OF ARTISTRY, TURMOIL, AND LEGACY

MARK C. WELLS

TABlE OF CONTENTS

INTRODUCTION

A guy who seemed to embody a thousand lives was reflected in the dim glimmer of the backstage mirror. In a silent homage to the several personalities that had sprung from his imagination into the screen, his fingertips traced the rim of a battered fedora that was lying on the bar. The weight of untold stories—stories of glory, tragedy, resiliency, and rebellion—was borne in his mysterious, profound eyes. Millions had been enthralled by those same eyes for years, but tonight they turned inward, seeking something more than the cheers.

A life lived on the brink of convention was hidden under the flash and glamour of Hollywood's spotlight. He was more than just a celebrity; he was a paradox, a contradiction in the form of charm. Few people really understood the man behind the mystique, but everyone knew his name. He moved fluidly between the quirky nature of pirates and the unadulterated compassion of troubled people for decades, dancing between fact and fancy. The reality of his journey, however, was still a mystery—a tapestry made up of strands of genius and disorder, victory and turmoil.

The throng outside screamed, relentlessly screaming his name. Supporters clutched posters, some featuring his favorite characters' recognizable smirks, while others paid homage to the renegade who didn't follow the rules. He represented disobedience in a society that pushed for conformity, and to them, he was a hero. However, what they saw on film was merely a small portion of the story, a window into the hectic existence that had molded the guy they loved.

He inhaled deeply as the curtain raised, entering a stage that had been transformed into a haven and a battleground. Despite the thunderous applause, he maintained his composure, and every motion he made was evidence of the years he had spent honing his trade. While the world attempted to write his own story for him, this was his arena, where he could immerse himself in the craft of storytelling.

When the cameras stopped rolling, though, who was he? What gave him the motivation to overcome all obstacles and become a worldwide celebrity? And how much did his unrelenting quest for authenticity cost him? A voyage as unpredictable as the man himself lay behind the well-crafted identities, the headlines, and the public spectacle.

This is the narrative of an artist who transformed his scars into works of art, a life lived without apology, and a tale of resiliency and reinvention. To comprehend him is to delve into the very core of creativity itself—to investigate a realm where suffering and ardor meet to produce a legacy that is unmatched. These pages contain the legend, the myth, and the guy. However, be advised that the truth is more nuanced, exquisite, and eerie than you may have thought.

CHAPTER 1: FROM KENTUCKY ROOTS TO HOLLYWOOD DREAMS

THE EARLY YEARS

Johnny Depp was born on June 9, 1963, in Owensboro, Kentucky, a tiny town distant from the glitter of Hollywood. Depp, the youngest of four siblings, was raised in a working-class household and was influenced by the difficulties of a nomadic upbringing. His parents, civil engineer John Christopher Depp and waitress Betty Sue Palmer, frequently found it difficult to give their kids stability. The family had relocated over twenty times by the time Depp was in his teens, finally settling in Miramar, Florida. He was exposed to a variety of experiences by these frequent moves, but they also made him feel dislocated and unrooted.

Depp had a restless and inquisitive nature from a young age, frequently withdrawing into his imagination to block out the chaos around him. His passion for music, which would serve as a pillar of his identity for the rest of his life, provided him with comfort. His mother gave him his first guitar when he was twelve years old. It became his constant companion and gave him a creative outlet for his feelings. Because of his passion for music, Depp formed garage bands with pals and briefly envisioned a career in rock and roll.

Depp did not, however, have an easy childhood. When he was fifteen, his parents' tumultuous marriage finally ended in divorce. He was severely impacted by the emotional strain of their separation and started acting out as a result of his inability to fit in. He left high school at the age of sixteen, initially to focus on his musical goals. Despite these difficulties, Depp's experiences at this time influenced the fortitude and self-reflection that would come to characterize his profession.

Depp joined a band named The Kids in his late teens, which helped his music career take off. The band had some success opening for well-known performers like the Ramones and Iggy Pop. The band moved to Los Angeles with the hopes of making a name for themselves. However, as is sometimes the case with artistic endeavors, success was elusive. Depp struggled to make ends meet and continued to pursue his dream of becoming a successful musician by taking on odd jobs, such as selling pens over the phone.

The unexpected turn in Depp's life occurred in Los Angeles. Depp met actor Nicolas Cage through makeup artist Lori Anne Allison, his ex-wife. Cage pushed the young musician to try acting because he sensed potential in him. After initially being dubious, Depp went to try out for a part in the low-budget horror movie *A Nightmare on Elm Street* (1984). He was shocked to get the role, and it was the start of an incredible career.

These early years prepared Depp for his future as an artist, even though his path to fame was still in its early stages. The depth and complexity that would eventually enthrall audiences across the world were influenced by his identity conflicts, love of music, and rebellious spirit. The Kentucky boy who had once aspired to be a rock star was set to make his debut in a world that would never forget his name.

CHASING THE DREAM

The path that Johnny Depp took to achieve his goals was not a simple one. It was characterized by diversions, disappointments, and an unwavering will that drove him to take chances and go against the grain. What started out as a desire to pursue a career in music would eventually turn into a profession that elevated him to the status of one of the most renowned and acclaimed actors of his generation. The path to stardom, however, was far from straightforward.

Following his high school graduation, Depp became deeply involved in the music industry. His love for the art form was clear in every note he played, and he felt that playing rock guitar was his genuine destiny. Depp dedicated himself to making music that spoke to the young people of the era with his band, The Kids. The Kids had a small fan base and even served as opening acts for well-known acts like the B-52s and the Talking Heads. But it didn't take long to realize how cruel the music business is. Despite their skill and commitment, the band had trouble landing a record deal, and Depp started to feel the effects of financial strain.

The kids' move to Los Angeles was meant to be the start of a lucrative music career. Rather, it turned into a time of reinvention and survival. Depp endured a great deal of rejection and disappointment while living in a tiny apartment and performing odd jobs to make ends meet. He characterized his work selling pens over the phone as soul-crushing, yet he held onto the belief that his big break was imminent. However, Depp started to wonder if music would ever give him the life he had imagined as the band started to lose steam.

During this uncertain period, fate stepped in. Nicolas Cage was introduced to Depp by his ex-wife, Lori Anne Allison. As a well-known actor, Cage recognized something special in Depp—undeveloped, undeveloped talent that might be brilliant on screen. At first, Depp rejected his advice that he should think about acting. With little to lose, he decided to give acting a try, even though it looked like a far cry from his dreams of becoming a rock star.

An important turning point was Depp's first tryout for the horror movie *A Nightmare on Elm Street* (1984). Despite his lack of formal training, the casting director was drawn to his charismatic personality and commanding presence. He made his cinematic debut when he was chosen to play the lead character's boyfriend, Glen. Despite its modest size, the part gave Depp a chance he had not previously explored.

Depp started to take acting more seriously after realizing that it would provide a fresh avenue for his artistic expression. He studied, refined his skills, and took on little parts in movies and TV shows. When he was chosen to play Officer Tom Hanson in the popular television series *21 Jump Street* in 1987, it was his big break. Nearly instantly, the show made Depp a teenage idol, providing him with the fame and financial security he had always desired.

But Depp didn't like being stereotyped as a pretty boy. Instead of merely being a face on a magazine cover, he aspired to be an artist. He made audacious career decisions, choosing parts in unconventional movies like *Edward Scissorhands* (1990) and *Cry-Baby* (1990), since he was determined not to be categorized. These roles demonstrated his range and solidified his reputation as a risk-taking, serious performer.

The fire that fed the dream had changed, but the dream itself had not. Depp had managed to transform his uniqueness and inventiveness into a new medium. With each part he played, he demonstrated that pursuing a dream required flexibility, tenacity, and self-truth rather than following a straight path. The hunt was far from over for Johnny Depp.

BREAKTHROUGH MOMENT

Every great career has a pivotal moment when timing, talent, and opportunity come together to produce something truly remarkable. That moment for Johnny Depp was his iconic performance in **Edward Scissorhands** (1990), a part that would forever alter the course of his career and solidify his status as one of Hollywood's most distinctive and gifted performers.

Depp was already well-known by the late 1980s because of his work on the television show **21 Jump Street**. Millions of people idolized him as a young heartthrob because to the show. Depp, however, was agitated. The clean-cut image the show had given him made him feel stuck, and he longed to break free from the limitations of traditional roles. Depp aspired to be an artist who could infuse his performances with nuance, passion, and depth rather than merely being another TV personality. His need for something new brought him together with Tim Burton, the innovative filmmaker who would go on to play a pivotal role in Depp's career.

It was obvious that Depp was taking on a job unlike any he had ever portrayed when he was chosen to play Edward Scissorhands. In contrast to Depp's reputation as a heartthrob, Edward was a kind, ethereal figure with scissors for hands. Vulnerability, subtlety, and the capacity to portray a wide range of emotions without primarily depending on speech were necessary for the character. Although it was a bold decision, Depp regarded it as the ideal chance to demonstrate his versatility as an actor.

Everyone on set was impacted by Depp's portrayal of the character because of its passion and sensitivity. He threw himself into Edward's world, using facial expressions and body language to convey the character's emotions, taking cues from silent movie stars like Charlie Chaplin. As a result, the performance was heartbreakingly tender and eerie. The loneliness, naiveté, and desire of an outsider attempting to make a connection with a society that didn't comprehend him were all encapsulated in Depp's portrayal of Edward.

Edward Scissorhands received widespread praise for its uniqueness and emotional depth, making it a critical and financial triumph. The movie demonstrated Depp's ability to select unusual parts that spoke to viewers more deeply in addition to showcasing his exceptional talent. Fans were enthralled by the vulnerability he brought to the film, while others applauded his ability to blend in with the role. Depp's transformation from a television actor to a powerful cinematic personality who could take on difficult and unusual roles began with the movie.

One of Hollywood's most enduring collaborations began with the work with Tim Burton. Together, Depp and Burton would produce a number of iconic movies that highlighted both Burton's distinctive visual storytelling and Depp's flexibility. Their collaborations on films like **Sleepy Hollow, Charlie and the Chocolate Factory,** and **Sweeney Todd** came to represent innovation and artistic daring.

Edward Scissorhands was a statement as much as a breakthrough for Depp. It sent a message to the world and Hollywood that Johnny Depp was not scared to break with convention and go against the grain. This position paved the way for a career marked by audacious decisions, ground-breaking performances, and a steadfast dedication to honesty. For Depp, the movie was more than just a career high point; it was the discovery of his creative voice, which would reverberate for many years to come.

CHAPTER 2: CRAFTING THE MISFIT – A CAREER IN CHARACTERS

THE RISE OF AN ICON

Following **Edward Scissorhands (1990)**, which was both critically and commercially successful, Johnny Depp's career took off. He differs from the stereotypical portrayal of traditional Hollywood leading males due to his special combination of talent, charisma, and risk-taking attitude. Over the course of the following ten years, Depp evolved from a promising actor into a symbol of cinematic genius, leaving behind a legacy characterized by adaptability, nuance, and a timeless attraction to viewers everywhere.

Depp chose assignments that stretched his skills and went against the grain rather than settling into roles that were predictable. He collaborated with well-known filmmakers in the early 1990s who shared his vision for unorthodox narrative. The films **Benny & Joon (1993)** and **What's Eating Gilbert Grape (1993)** showcased his talent for portraying characters who are thoughtful and sympathetic. These parts showcased a side of Depp that both critics and viewers loved—an actor who wasn't scared to deviate from the formula of the blockbuster to tackle stories full of nuance and humanity.

His roles became more varied as his reputation for subtle performances increased. With roles like **Ed Wood (1994),** in which he portrayed the eccentric and driven director who produced some of Hollywood's most notorious cult films, Depp and director Tim Burton's partnership grew even more. The part demonstrated Depp's comedic timing and his capacity to empathetically portray quirky, fantastical characters. Even though the movie wasn't a box office success, Depp's performance received high appreciation, which strengthened his reputation as an actor who isn't afraid to try new things.

With roles that were more dramatic and dark, Depp further demonstrated his flexibility. He co starred with Al Pacino as an FBI undercover agent who infiltrated the mob in **Donnie Brasco (1997)**. He was praised for his ability to compete with acting greats in this gritty crime drama, which showcased another aspect of his abilities. The part also demonstrated Depp's ability to succeed in more conventional Hollywood genres while keeping his own style.

Depp never pursued popularity for its own reason, even in the face of his critical triumph. His appeal was only increased by his unwillingness to follow Hollywood conventions. He turned into a rebel who cherished narrative over fame and a symbol of artistic integrity. A generation of admirers who respected his refusal to compromise authenticity for fame found resonance in this philosophy. As he kept his personal life largely quiet and concentrated on his art and creative pursuits, Depp's mystique grew.

Additional partnerships with forward-thinking filmmakers such as Terry Gilliam (**Fear and Loathing in Las Vegas, 1998**) and Roman Polanski (**The Ninth Gate, 1999**) emerged in the late 1990s. Depp further cemented his reputation as an artist who isn't afraid to push boundaries by showcasing his ability to handle bizarre, thought-provoking themes in each part.

Depp became well-known by the early **2000s**, when he was praised for taking chances and giving characters life that others may have written off as being too odd or difficult. He was more than just an actor; he was a cultural figure who changed the definition of what it meant to be a Hollywood star. His ascent was characterized by his dedication to a single artistic vision rather than by following fads or expectations.

With the start of the new millennium, Depp's career was on the verge of another change. His unorthodox decisions had set the stage for a trip that would eventually propel him into international prominence with the debut of a certain intrepid pirate, a part that would permanently alter his place in movie history. But despite his growing popularity, Depp never wavered in his commitment to telling stories, making sure that every performance—no matter how big or small—reflected the nuance and complexity that had come to characterize him. In addition to becoming a successful actor, Johnny Depp's rise marked the beginning of an iconic figure whose impact would extend well beyond the movie theater.

BLOCKBUSTERS AND INDIE GEMS

A unique combination of independent masterpieces and box office successes throughout his career has shaped Johnny Depp's reputation as one of Hollywood's most adaptable and daring actors. Depp's decisions, which range from obscure, art-house movies to popular franchises, show his unwavering ambition to explore a variety of people and stories without being constrained by commercial norms.

The Blockbuster Era

Disney's **Pirates of the Caribbean: The Curse of the Black Pearl** marked the beginning of Depp's journey into the world of enormous financial success in **2003**. His portrayal of rock star Keith Richards's flamboyant, swaggering pirate Captain Jack Sparrow was a revelation. Depp gave the role a unique personality that enthralled viewers and led to his first Academy Award nomination by infusing it with charm and weirdness. Depp's reputation as a worldwide superstar was cemented when the film, which made over $650 million worldwide, gave rise to a franchise that would eventually feature five sequels.

Depp's career took a significant shift with the **Pirates of the Caribbean** series. It demonstrated his capacity to lead a blockbuster while upholding his renowned dedication to uniqueness. One of the most recognizable figures in movie history, Captain Jack Sparrow is adored for his humor, unpredictable nature, and subtle sensitivity. The franchise gave Depp enormous recognition and financial success, but it also showed that he could make a lasting creative impression in even the most commercial endeavors.

Depp maintained his ability to strike a balance between big-budget jobs and artistic integrity after the success of **Pirates of the Caribbean**. Tim Burton-directed movies like **Charlie and the Chocolate Factory (2005)** and **Alice in Wonderland (2010)** gave Depp the chance to add his distinct style to fantasy settings. These movies were huge box office successes; **Alice in Wonderland** brought in over $1 billion worldwide. Depp demonstrated his ability to give even the most outlandish creatures a profoundly human quality with his whimsical yet melancholic portrayal of the Mad Hatter.

A Dedication to Independent Treasures

Depp never gave up on his love of indie films, even after achieving fame in the mainstream industry. He looked for opportunities to take on challenging, non-traditional tasks throughout his career. Terry Gilliam's **Fear and Loathing in Las Vegas (1998)** was one such movie. In the movie, which was based on Hunter S. Thompson's book, Depp played journalist Raoul Duke's drug-fueled anarchy. Despite critics' disagreements, the movie became a cult favorite because of Depp's daring and transformational performance.

Additionally, Depp excelled in the moving drama **Finding Neverland (2004),** which focused on the author of **Peter Pan,** J.M. Barrie. Depp received another Academy Award nomination for the portrayal, which revealed a softer, more subdued side of him. His depiction of Barrie's battle to strike a balance between fantasy and reality struck a profound chord with viewers, serving as a reminder of Depp's unmatched capacity to inspire awe and empathy.

Tim Burton and Depp reunited in **Ed Wood (1994)** to narrate the tale of one of Hollywood's most notorious directors. Depp's portrayal of the colorful, upbeat Ed Wood was a master tutorial in appreciating eccentricity. Despite not being a box office hit, the movie received a lot of praise for its heart and humor, which cemented Depp's status as an actor who doesn't hesitate to try something new.

Observing the Line

Depp's ability to succeed in both the indie and blockbuster genres without sacrificing his artistic personality is maybe what makes his career so exceptional. One minute he may be the star of a multibillion-dollar franchise, and the next he could be a tortured poet in **The Libertine (2004)**. He stood out as an artist with a distinct vision because of his dedication to presenting stories, regardless of funding or audience size.

His profound regard for teamwork was also evident in this contradiction. Whether collaborating with great filmmakers such as Jim Jarmusch, Gore Verbinski, or Tim Burton, Depp always gave it his all and infused each production with enthusiasm and originality. Every movie, whether it was an independent passion project or a Hollywood blockbuster, had his distinctive mark because of his willingness to take chances and defy expectations.

In addition to demonstrating his flexibility, Johnny Depp's career in both blockbusters and independent jewels is a celebration of a performer who defies convention. Whether Depp's work moves people with a quiet, reflective character or entertains millions with a famous pirate, it never fails to serve as a potent reminder of the power of storytelling in all its forms.

MASTER OF

TRANSFORMATION

Johnny Depp's ability to fully immerse himself in his roles is one of his most distinctive acting qualities. Because he has embraced characters who require emotional, psychological, and physical changes, he has come to represent transition over the years. Depp is one of the most varied and captivating actors in film because of his dedication to completely embodying his roles, whether it be through intricate makeup, quirky costumes, or incredibly nuanced performances.

The Craft of Transformation

Early in his career, Depp's ability to transform was clear. He created an otherworldly persona in **Edward Scissorhands (1990)** that combined desire, tenderness, and innocence. Edward's discomfort and infantile amazement were captured by Depp's performance, which depended more on subtle physique than language. Depp's unrecognizable pale makeup, untamed black hair, and scissor-wielding hands demonstrated his commitment to embodying the role rather than just portraying it.

This method became a defining characteristic of Depp's work. His ability to alter was further demonstrated by his partnerships with forward-thinking filmmakers such as Tim Burton. Depp played the quirky, upbeat director in **Ed Wood (1994)** with a contagious energy that struck a mix between humor and tragedy. Beyond just playing the part, Depp immersed himself in it, meticulously imitating the voice and mannerisms of the real Ed Wood by watching old video of him.

Physical Change

Depp has continuously accepted parts that require drastic physical transformations, frequently spending hours applying prosthetics and makeup to make his personas come to life. He reimagined the mysterious Willy Wonka in **Charlie and the Chocolate Factory (2005),** giving her a high-pitched, unnervingly happy manner and a pale, nearly doll-like visage. Although controversial, his interpretation was unquestionably unique and showed his willingness to take chances.

His portrayal of Captain Jack Sparrow in **Pirates of the Caribbean: The Curse of the Black Pearl (2003)** may have been his most famous metamorphosis. In order to create a figure that was equal parts rock star and pirate, Depp recreated the classic swashbuckler by drawing inspiration from rock hero Keith Richards. Sparrow's colorful clothing design, slurred speech, and exaggerated gestures established him a cultural phenomenon and demonstrated that Depp could create incredibly unique characters in popular blockbusters.

Depp's portrayal as the Mad Hatter in **Alice in Wonderland (2010)** called for a wide range of emotions, from whimsical to sorrowful. Depp once again became a character who looked to have been taken directly out of a storybook thanks to his vibrant makeup, large eyes (made possible by computer-generated imagery), and his remarkable ability to capture eccentricity. The Mad Hatter stood out in a visually spectacular movie because of his ability to strike a balance between the ridiculous and the meaningful.

Emotional Complexity and Depth

Depp frequently explores his characters' psychological depths through his transformations, which go beyond the physical. He portrayed **Peter Pan's** author, J.M. Barrie, in **Finding Neverland (2004)** with a subdued intensity that emphasized the character's contemplative nature and limitless imagination. In contrast to his more extravagant parts, this performance demonstrated Depp's talent for subtly and subtly expressing emotion.

Depp played the part of a violent barber driven by a desire for vengeance in **Sweeney Todd: The Demon Barber of Fleet Street (2007).** Despite his sinister actions, he portrayed the character with a haunting vulnerability that made his portrayal both operatic and terrifying. Depp showcased his versatility by singing for the first time in a major motion picture, fully engrossed in the Gothic ambiance of the narrative.

Depp performed one of his most terrifying turns as Boston mobster Whitey Bulger in the **2015** film **Black Mass**. Depp was almost unrecognizable with his icy blue contact lenses, slicked-back hair, and a pale, threatening face. His portrayal, which captured Bulger's deliberate brutality and alluded to the inner complexity that motivated him, was commended for its ferocity.

A Transformation-Based Career

Depp's appreciation for narrative and his willingness to push the envelope are the foundations of his ability to transform into characters. He sees acting as a kind of artistic expression that requires complete focus and commitment. Because of this dedication, he has become a darling among filmmakers as well as a source of interest for viewers who are always curious about what he will do next.

Depp's shifts go beyond makeup and costume, whether he's portraying a crafty criminal, a vindictive barber, or a playful owner of a chocolate factory. His characters become living, breathing manifestations of his creative energy because he gives them his whole self. He is one of the most dynamic performers of his time, and his ability to transform is not just a testament to his talent but also a distinguishing characteristic of his career.

Because of his readiness to embrace change, Johnny Depp has become a symbol of artistic bravery in a field that frequently rewards conformity. His performances serve as a reminder to audiences of the potential of reinvention, demonstrating that an actor can become anything—and anyone—with enough creativity and commitment.

CHAPTER 3: THE PIRATES' CAPTAIN – DEFINING JACK SPARROW

BIRTH OF A CULTURASPARRO

The narrative of Johnny Depp's transformation from a disobedient kid in Kentucky to one of the most cherished cultural icons of our day is one of audacious decisions, limitless imagination, and a steadfast dedication to authenticity. As someone who has consistently reinterpreted what it means to be a Hollywood celebrity, Depp is more than just an actor. His ascent to popularity is not the only factor contributing to his status as a cultural icon; he has also had a significant influence on fashion, art, audiences, and the storytelling trade itself.

Breaking Through the Conventional Mold

Depp made a name for himself in a field that is sometimes dominated by typecasting and formulas. Early in his career, he defied the stereotype of a Hollywood leading man by choosing complicated, unusual characters over jobs that were sure to be predictable. Depp became increasingly disillusioned with the one-dimensional roles that were being presented to him after his breakthrough performance in **21 Jump Street**, where he was cast as a teenage heartthrob. He took a risk by looking for projects that spoke to his creative sensibilities rather than following the trend of popular stardom.

This choice not only distinguished him but also solidified his standing as a risk-taking actor. Movies like **Edward Scissorhands (1990), Benny & Joon (1993), and Ed Wood (1994)** demonstrated his talent for giving quirky characters nuance and sympathy. Audiences responded favorably to Depp's emphasis on authenticity above commercial appeal because they recognized in him a parallel to their wish to defy expectations.

Changing the Meaning of Stardom

The popularity of Johnny Depp mirrored a change in Hollywood society as viewers started to appreciate performers who were honest and unique in their parts. As an actor who embraced the strange, the fantastical, and the whimsical rather than playing it safe, he came to represent this new wave. His image as an artist who flourished in creative, avant-garde projects was further enhanced by his partnerships with directors such as Terry Gilliam and Tim Burton.

However, he became an icon for reasons other than his filmography. Another important factor was Depp's personal style and off-screen character. Depp became a trailblazer with his diverse style, which combined rock-star flair, vintage boho, and subtle elegance. He established himself as a cultural tastemaker and influenced a generation of devotees with his wide-brimmed hats, layered necklaces, and love of scarves. Depp lived his parts, integrating them into a broader story of uniqueness and self-expression, rather than merely playing them.

The Influence of Classic Roles

Some of Depp's personas went beyond the realm of film to become cultural icons. Perhaps the most well-known example is Captain Jack Sparrow, the daring antihero of Disney's **Pirates of the Caribbean** franchise. Depp's portrayal of Sparrow was a celebration of quirkiness as well as a reimagining of the pirate image. Children and adults alike found Sparrow to be a cherished character due to his intoxicated swagger, slurred speech, and unpredictable charm.

Captain Jack Sparrow was a cultural phenomenon rather than just a part. Depp gained admirers worldwide due to the character's success, which elevated him to a degree of international fame that few performers could match. Adults cited Sparrow's comments, kids dressed up as him for Halloween, and his image became a mainstay of pop culture in general, theme parks, and products. Nevertheless, Depp stuck to his creative values despite this enormous commercial success, making Sparrow as complex and distinctive as any of his other parts.

Impact Outside of the Screen

Depp's influence goes well beyond his work in movies. His courageous dedication to his work has served as an inspiration to innumerable performers, artists, and creators. He is a shining example for people who appreciate uniqueness and innovation because of his readiness to take on positions that others would be afraid to take. In order to leave a more comprehensive artistic legacy, Depp has also worked with writers, painters, and musicians, using his position to promote their work.

His rock-star persona has become an essential part of his character, and his influence is similarly felt in the music industry. Alongside icons like Alice Cooper and Joe Perry, Depp has collaborated with bands like Hollywood Vampires, showcasing his versatility as a performer and his enduring passion for music. His appeal as a versatile cultural icon is further cemented by the crossover between acting and music.

A Durable Heritage

The fact that Johnny Depp became a cultural icon is evidence of his sincerity and defiance of social norms. He has demonstrated that becoming a true celebrity means embracing uniqueness and telling important tales rather than playing it safe or adhering to trends. Depp has a profound impact on fans' lives outside of Hollywood, serving as a reminder that it's acceptable to be unique and that self-expression should not be sacrificed for success.

Johnny Depp is now more than just an actor; he is a representation of creative bravery and uniqueness. A new generation of artists and visionaries is still motivated by his legacy, demonstrating that those who dare to be extraordinary create idols rather than them being born.

BEHIND THE SCENES

Millions have been captivated by Johnny Depp's on-screen persona, but the backstage tales of his life and career tell an equally captivating tale. From his painstaking preparation for parts to his dealings with crew members, directors, and co-stars, Depp's off-screen persona portrays a multifaceted, devoted, and frequently mysterious person. His unconventional demeanor and acting style have influenced not only his performances but also the atmosphere of his movie sets.

The Process That Creates the Magic

Depp is well known for his meticulous acting technique. He does more than just portray a character; he takes on the role, exploring their motivations, history, and innermost thoughts. He puts a lot of effort into his study for each part, frequently working with directors, makeup artists, and costume designers to create a unique appearance and feel for his character.

In **Edward Scissorhands (1990),** Depp made up for the character's lack of verbal communication by using subtle body and emotional expression to portray Edward's naivete and desire. He worked closely with filmmaker Tim Burton to perfect Edward's visual appearance, including the recognizable scissor hands and gothic-inspired makeup, and he studied mime techniques to convey ideas through movement.

Depp allegedly based Captain Jack Sparrow on Rolling Stones guitarist Keith Richards for the 2003 film **Pirates of the Caribbean: The Curse of the Black Pearl.** By researching historical narratives and assimilating a characteristically flamboyant, nearly inebriated swagger into the character's mannerisms and walk, Depp immersed himself in pirate culture. As a result, Disney executives were first perplexed by the performance's uniqueness and questioned its eccentricity. Depp, however, persisted in his faith in his creative vision, and history validated this belief.

Partnerships and Associations

Depp's long-lasting collaborations with filmmakers such as Terry Gilliam, Gore Verbinski, and Tim Burton have become legendary. One of the most fruitful actor-director partnerships in contemporary filmmaking was forged by Depp and Burton. Famous movies like **Edward Scissorhands, Sleepy Hollow (1999), and Sweeney Todd: The Demon Barber of Fleet Street (2007)** resulted from their mutual appreciation of the macabre and the whimsical. Depp, whom Burton frequently referred to as his muse, was able to vividly and imaginatively realize his fantastical dreams.

Behind the scenes, Depp is renowned for his friendship and commitment to his staff and other actors. He frequently goes above and above to make people feel at ease on set and is known for being kind and affable. Despite the demanding schedule, Depp would regularly engage with the crew during filming **Pirates of the Caribbean**, exchanging stories and jokes and fostering a sense of camaraderie.

Depp also grew close to his younger co-stars. His relationship with Freddie Highmore during the filming of **Charlie and the**

Chocolate Factory (2005) and Finding Neverland (2004) demonstrated his loving nature as he provided the young actor with encouragement and direction. He also demonstrated his ability to relate to actors of all ages on the set of **Sherlock Gnomes (2018)** through his relationship with young actor Millie Bobby Brown.

A Playground for Actors

Depp is frequently characterized as an actor who enjoys working with others and trying new things. He continuously improvises and tests out new concepts on the set, seeing it as a creative playground. Depp's spontaneous improvisations during rehearsals gave rise to several of Captain Jack Sparrow's eccentricities, such as his odd hand motions and slurred speech. He is a favorite among directors who value his unpredictable nature because of his willingness to take chances and defy accepted character representations.

But there are drawbacks to this inventiveness. Occasionally, Depp's tendency to push limits has produced conflict with producers and studio executives who might not immediately understand his vision. Nonetheless, people who have collaborated with him frequently commend his commitment and the genuineness he brings to every position.

Outside the Camera

Depp's life off-screen has been as diverse and outlandish as his acting career. Known for his strange interests and varied inclinations, he frequently paints or plays the guitar in his spare time on set. Depp's love of music regularly permeates his professional life; he has entertained the cast and crew with spontaneous jam sessions.

Additionally, Depp has a track record of generosity and generosity. He notably dressed up as Captain Jack Sparrow during the filming in England and went to children's hospitals to cheer up little fans. These unplanned deeds of kindness have come to define Depp's off-screen demeanor, exposing a side of him that is as kind and sympathetic as it is mysterious.

The Difficulties of Being Famous

Depp's life behind the scenes has not been without its challenges, despite the inventiveness and friendship. His career has sometimes been clouded by the tremendous strain of popularity combined with personal struggles. Nevertheless, Depp has remained dedicated to his art despite hardship. He uses his experiences as a source of emotional depth and genuineness in his performances.

On-Set Legacy

Like the personas he creates, Johnny Depp's backstage persona is interesting. He is an artist who leaves a lasting impression on everyone he works with and who thrives on connection, creativity, and teamwork. According to Depp, the wonder of filmmaking lies not only in what takes place in front of the camera but also in the connections, dangers, and unwavering search for the artistic truth that lies behind it.

He has gained the admiration of both fans and peers for his ability to strike a balance between the demands of his profession and his inherent humanism. Whether he's wearing a pirate's helmet, using a barber's razor, or vanishing into a fantastical Burton-like universe, Depp's backstage narrative is one of commitment, artistry, and a love for making the fantastical come to life.

THE LEGACY OF THE CARIBBEAN

In addition to redefining Johnny Depp's career, his performance as Captain Jack Sparrow in *Pirates of the Caribbean: The Curse of the Black Pearl* (2003) had a lasting impact on popular culture around the world. Depp turned a goofy pirate into one of the most recognizable characters in movie history throughout five films and almost two decades. At its core was the naughty, erratic, and utterly endearing Captain Jack Sparrow, who helped the *Pirates of the Caribbean* franchise become a global phenomenon by fusing exciting storytelling with enduring characters.

Reimagining the Pirate Persona

Few anticipated that a pirate movie would be a box office hit when **The Curse of the Black Pearl** was first revealed. Pirate-themed films were viewed as a financial risk, and the genre had largely lost popularity. But the tide was changed by Johnny Depp's inventive portrayal of Jack Sparrow. Depp envisioned Jack as a swaggering, slightly insane antihero who marched to his drum, drawing inspiration from rock legend Keith Richards.

To put it mildly, Depp's performance was out of the ordinary. Disney officials were originally confused by his slurred speech, strange demeanor, and flamboyant style, fearing that viewers would not identify with such a peculiar lead character. Depp, however, remained steadfast in his belief that Sparrow would stand out due to his oddities. His intuition was right—Captain Jack Sparrow swiftly emerged as the franchise's defining characteristic, securing Depp a nomination for Best Actor at the Academy Awards and solidifying his place as a worldwide icon.

An Event of Culture

Dead Man's Chest (2006), At World's End (2007), On Stranger Tides (2011), and Dead Men Tell No Tales (2017) are the four sequels to the popular film The Curse of the Black Pearl. With a combined box office total of billions, **Pirates of the Caribbean** is one of the most successful franchises in movie history.

Jack Sparrow, a figure who went beyond the screen to become a cultural icon, was at the heart of it all. His eccentric charisma won him admirers worldwide, and his catchphrases—such as "Savvy?"—became commonplace.

With his dreadlocks, tricorn hat, and many baubles, Sparrow's unique appearance served as the inspiration for innumerable Halloween costumes, cosplay ensembles, and souvenirs.

Jack Sparrow's influence went beyond the actual movies. By transforming the historically somber topic of piracy into a source of laughter, adventure, and amazement, Depp's interpretation gave the idea fresh life. Sparrow was added to theme park attractions, and stories of daring exploits on the high seas captivated children's imaginations.

A World Ambassador

Acting was only one aspect of Depp's relationship with the role. He adopted the character of Jack Sparrow in real life over the years, dressing up as the character for charity functions, public appearances, and hospital stays. In one particularly memorable moment, he surprised guests at Disneyland by playing Sparrow and chatting with them on the **Pirates of the Caribbean** ride.

These actions helped to bridge the gap between fantasy and reality and cemented Depp's reputation as a global spokesperson for the franchise. For millions of fans, Johnny

Depp **was** Captain Jack Sparrow, not just a pirate. He became a well-liked personality all around the world because of his commitment to making supporters happy, especially kids.

Jack Sparrow's Development

Depp kept developing Jack Sparrow's character throughout the series, giving his cunning, self-centered nature more nuance. While **At World's End** examined Jack's tense connections with both friends and enemies, **Dead Man's Chest** gave viewers hints of his frailty and fear of dying. Throughout several movies, Sparrow remained captivating due to Depp's ability to strike a mix of humor and emotional depth.

Depp's acting was still a standout, even in the less well-reviewed films. His dedication to the part guaranteed that Sparrow would always be the focal point of the show, a figure whose capricious antics delighted viewers irrespective of the plot.

Legacy and Impact

Beyond its financial success, **Pirates of the Caribbean** has left a lasting legacy. The franchise brought the pirate genre back to life and spawned a flurry of media with a pirate theme, ranging from video games and novels to movies and TV series. Its fusion of action, humor, and mystical aspects served as a model for contemporary adventure movies, and inspiring series such as **Guardians of the Galaxy.**

Captain Jack Sparrow became a pivotal part of Johnny Depp's career, showcasing his capacity to transcend expectations and take creative risks. His ability as an actor and his determination to push boundaries are demonstrated by the role, which continues to be a touchstone of his career.

A Difficult Chapter

The franchise has encountered difficulties in recent years, such as debates about reviving the series with a different cast and scandals involving Depp's personal life. The significance of Depp's contribution to the **Pirates of the Caribbean** legacy has not been lessened, even though these events have generated discussion among both fans and critics.

Many people can't imagine Captain Jack Sparrow without Johnny Depp, whose distinct vision and talent made the role come to life. Regardless of the franchise's continuation, Sparrow will always hold a special position in movie history as a representation of bravery, tenacity, and the strength of individualism.

The Lasting Enchantment

Johnny Depp's portrayal of Captain Jack Sparrow in the **Pirates of the Caribbean** the franchise will go down in history as one of the greatest motion picture productions of the twenty-first century. Fans are reminded of the fun, wonder, and unpredictable nature Johnny Depp brought to the high seas by the Caribbean's enduring magic. The legend of Captain Jack Sparrow endures from the Black Pearl to the most remote regions of the globe, driven by the actor's creativity and bravery in redefining what it means to be a pirate.

CHAPTER 4: THE PUBLIC AND PRIVATE JOHNNY

A MEDIA OBSESSION

For decades, Johnny Depp's life and work have been scrutinized by the public and media, with news outlets worldwide covering his every action, from career victories to personal struggles. Few celebrities have had to deal with the extreme level of attention and conjecture that Depp has, and even fewer have been able to handle it with the fortitude that he has. He has had a two-pronged connection with the media, which has helped him become a superstar while also subjecting him to constant scrutiny, sensationalism, and criticism.

How to Become a Media Star

Depp immediately became popular among both fans and journalists due to his unique charisma and captivating appearance. His intriguing nature, rebellious attitude, and brooding good looks captivated the press early in his career. The mystery around him was only increased by his appearances in movies like **Edward Scissorhands (1990)** and **Donnie Brasco (1997),** in which he frequently portrayed characters that reflected his own complicated, outsider identity.

During these formative years, Depp and the media had a generally mutually beneficial relationship. He was hailed in Hollywood as an actor who bucked the conventional leading-man paradigm and as having a distinct and genuine voice. He was portrayed as a heartthrob with a depth that distinguished him from his contemporaries in magazine covers, interviews, and photo spreads. Depp's reputation as a real artist rather than simply another movie star was further solidified by his frank interviews in which he discussed his love of art and contempt for fame.

A Target for Tabloids

The media's interest in Depp's private life increased along with his fame. The media relentlessly documented his high-profile romances with celebrities like Kate Moss and Winona Ryder, turning them into tabloid fodder. The notorious "Winona Forever" tattoo, which he later changed to "Wino Forever" following their split, came to represent the media's obsession with his love life.

Although not for the reasons he may have wanted, Depp's later marriage to actress Amber Heard thrust him into even greater prominence. Their turbulent relationship and well-publicized legal disputes turned into one of the 21st century's most extensively reported celebrity scandals. With news organizations, social media, and fans scrutinizing every detail, the media flurry around their court battles transformed Depp's hardships into a public spectacle.

The relationship between Depp and the media underwent a sea change during this time. He became the focus of divisive narratives, with some media sources depicting him as a villain and others as a victim, after once being a favorite of the press. The coverage went well beyond the entertainment sections and turned into a hot topic in conversations about accountability, abuse, and the influence of public opinion.

Social Media's Function

The media's fixation on Johnny Depp was intensified by the emergence of social media. His character became the subject of heated discussions on social media sites like Twitter, Instagram, and YouTube, where both supporters and detractors used hashtags, memes, and viral videos to express their views. Millions of people watched Depp's court battles with Heard livestreamed and evaluated in real-time, much like a major play.

This phenomenon of the digital age demonstrated how celebrity culture is changing and how traditional media channels are no longer the only ones influencing public opinion. Supporters of Depp, united under slogans such as "Justice for Johnny," rallied around him on social media by posting testimonials, supporting documentation, and heartfelt pleas. His critics, meanwhile, used the same venues to cast doubt on his deeds and condemn his conduct.

The Cost of Notoriety

The constant attention from the media has cost Depp dearly. His artistic accomplishments have frequently been overshadowed by the examination of his personal life, turning a legendary career into a string of headlines and catchphrases. Depp has publicly discussed the toll that this has taken on him, calling celebrity a "monster" that eats up solitude and warps reality.

Depp has demonstrated incredible fortitude in the face of these difficulties, turning to his art as a haven and a vehicle for self-expression. While juggling the demands of public life, he has persisted in working on passion projects, collaborating with forward-thinking filmmakers, and pursuing his love of music.

A Difficult Legacy

The media's infatuation with Johnny Depp is evidence of both his timeless appeal and the complexity of his character. Whether it is his transforming performances, his distinct style, or his turbulent personal life, he is a figure that provokes powerful reactions. For better or worse, the public's view of Depp has been greatly influenced by the media, which has made him a representation of both the glamour and the darker aspects of Hollywood.

Looking Ahead

The media is still a constant influence in Depp's life as he works to restore his career and rewrite his story. Some media sites have started to highlight his creative accomplishments and charitable endeavors, while others are still obsessed with the scandals that have plagued him. For both fans and critics, Johnny Depp's tale is far from over, and as he continues to negotiate the challenges of celebrity, artistry, and humanity, the media's position in it is probably going to change.

The media's portrayal of Johnny Depp's life serves as a warning about the cost of fame and the influence of perception. However, it also demonstrates his tenacity and unwavering dedication to his art, serving as a reminder that beneath the news is a guy who is still mysterious and alluring.

LOVE, LOSS, AND FAMILY

Love, death, and family have all had a significant impact on Johnny Depp's life, both personally and professionally. Behind the scenes, there is a web of relationships that have had a significant impact on both the artist and the man, even though his public persona frequently displays his alluring charm and strangeness. Depp's personal life illustrates the intricacies of love, the anguish of loss, and the enduring power of familial ties via everything from romantic relationships and heartbreaks to his unwavering dedication as a parent.

The Family's Origins

Depp's childhood in Owensboro, Kentucky, shaped his views on family and love. Depp, who was born on June 9, 1963, was the youngest of four siblings in a family that frequently experienced emotional upheaval and financial hardship. When Johnny was only a teenager, his parents, John Christopher Depp and Betty Sue Palmer, got divorced. Depp's ideas on stability and relationships were profoundly shaped by the breakup of his marriage and the repeated migrations he experienced as a child.

Despite the difficulties, Depp frequently attributes his strong will and inventive energy to his mother, Betty Sue. Depp's work ethic was greatly impacted by Betty's perseverance, as she worked relentlessly as a waitress to provide for her family. However, there were conflicts in their relationship because of Betty's rigid and even erratic behavior. Depp publicly characterized her eventual death in 2016 as a traumatic experience that was indicative of the complexity of their relationship.

A Romantic Rollercoaster

As turbulent and colorful as his profession, Johnny Depp's love life has been characterized by high-profile partnerships and public splits that frequently turned into tabloid spectacles. Although brief, his first marriage—to makeup artist Lori Anne Allison in 1983—was noteworthy. Depp's career was greatly aided by Lori, who through her contacts exposed him to the entertainment industry.

The media's interest in his relationships increased along with his notoriety. During the early 1990s, Depp and actress Winona Ryder had one of Hollywood's most famous relationships. The pair fell in love right away after meeting on the set of *Edward Scissorhands* (1990). The renowned phrase "Winona Forever," which represents their close bond, was inked on Depp's arm. Depp was devastated when their relationship ended due to the demands of celebrity and their youth.

Later on in life, Depp started a passionate and erratic relationship with supermodel Kate Moss. Their brief romance, which featured both their glitzy moments and their furious disagreements, took center stage in the media. Even though they broke up in 1997, they have since spoken well of one another.

Depp's collaboration with French singer and actress Vanessa Paradis was one of his longest-lasting relationships. After meeting in 1998, the couple stayed out of the spotlight for 14 years while raising their two kids, Lily-Rose and Jack. Their years together were a time of security and domestic joy, and Depp frequently referred to Vanessa as his anchor. Even though their love relationship ended in 2012, the two have remained respectful of one another and have a solid co-parenting relationship.

The Anguish of Death

Significant losses have also occurred in Depp's personal life, including the death of close friends and the breakup of important relationships. Depp, who was in the Viper Room on the night of River Phoenix's terrible overdose in 1993, was profoundly impacted by the actor and musician's passing. Depp's ideas on death and the transient nature of life were impacted by this tragedy as well as the demands of celebrity, which drove him deeper into reflection.

Another type of loss for Depp was the legal and personal struggles he had with actress Amber Heard, which started after their brief marriage. Their relationship's public backlash and the resulting legal disputes presented significant obstacles on both a personal and professional level. Although the media craze around their court battles was emotionally draining, Depp took comfort in his family's and his fans' steadfast support.

Fatherhood: A Joyful Experience

Depp has continuously found stability and meaning in his role as a father amidst the turmoil of his public life. His world has revolved around his kids, John "Jack" Christopher Depp III and Lily-Rose Melody Depp. Depp has frequently discussed how becoming a father changed him, giving him a stronger sense of duty and a fresh outlook on life.

Depp is close to Lily-Rose, who has a successful acting and modeling career that follows in her father's footsteps. While preserving her anonymity, he has taken satisfaction in her accomplishments. In a similar vein, Depp and his son Jack have a loving and respectful relationship. Depp cherishes their time together and the peaceful moments that come with being a family, while Jack has mostly avoided the spotlight.

The Lasting Connections

Love, loss, and family are not discrete events for Johnny Depp; rather, they are interwoven themes that shape his path. His personal and familial ties have influenced his outlook on life and given his artwork a deeper emotional dimension. Through the joys of motherhood, the heartache of bereavement, or the highs of being in love, Depp has found inspiration and strength in those closest to him.

These events are echoes that reverberate throughout his work rather than being just discrete episodes in his personal life. The lessons he's learned from love and sorrow are frequently reflected in the complexity and vulnerability he gives to his roles. Furthermore, his strong bond with his family is what characterizes him, even though the media may highlight the more dramatic parts of his personal life.

Love, loss, and family are both obstacles and pillars in the larger story of Johnny Depp's life, reminding us of the persona behind the star. Depp perseveres through it all, finding comfort and purpose in the most important connections.

THE PRICE OF FAME

Millions of people adored Johnny Depp, and his quick ascent to fame brought him fortune and influence. However, celebrity has two sides, and for Depp, the negative aspects of it frequently outweighed the positive ones. Being one of Hollywood's most mysterious characters, he has suffered greatly from the pressures of being in the spotlight, where his private problems, scandals, and errors were magnified for the world to witness. "The price of fame," as Depp has mentioned in interviews, is not only the loss of privacy but also the almost continual scrutiny and criticism that accompany it.

The Charm of Celebrity

Fame was a far-off and elusive idea when Depp initially started working in the entertainment business. His first goal was to pursue music rather than acting, and he ended himself in Hollywood more by accident than on purpose. However, Depp shot to fame in the late 1980s after securing his breakthrough role on the television series *21 Jump Street*. Young, defiant, and incredibly attractive, he rose to fame fast and was adored by millions of people.

Depp, however, was never at ease with this degree of scrutiny. Depp defied the stereotype of the typical Hollywood star, even though many people in his situation may have adopted the lifestyle of a celebrity. He resented being labeled a "pretty boy" and aggressively pursued parts that went against how most people saw him. He received praise from critics for his rebellious nature, but it also put him in danger of running afoul of the expectations of celebrity.

The Privacy Gap

Depp's privacy was one of the first things to suffer as a result of his stardom. The public and media were privy to Depp's life from his early days as a rising star to his current position as one of Hollywood's most well-known figures. Every endeavor, every relationship, and every mistake was examined, analyzed, and reported in tabloids.

In particular, his sexual relationships were under constant public scrutiny. The media made Depp's romantic life a spectacle, whether it was his brief affair with Winona Ryder, his turbulent relationship with Kate Moss, or his long-term alliance with Vanessa Paradis. Even after becoming a parent, Depp found it difficult to protect his kids from the prying eyes of paparazzi, who frequently stalked his family in an attempt to find the next big story.

Depp's final years were as difficult. His well-publicized legal disputes with his ex-wife Amber Heard brought to light very private facets of his life. With millions of supporters and detractors watching every development, the court cases—which were extensively covered and discussed—became a worldwide media event. For Depp, it served as a sobering reminder of how celebrities can turn personal hardships into amusement for the general public.

The Expectation's Weight

Additionally, fame came with a heavy weight of expectations. Being one of Hollywood's most lucrative celebrities, Depp was always under pressure to give standout performances and uphold his reputation as a dependable and adaptable performer. He successfully tackled this task for years, giving memorable performances in movies like *Pirates of the Caribbean*, *Edward Scissorhands*, and *Sweeney Todd*.

But the same success that made him famous throughout the world also made his work more closely examined. As his reputation developed, listeners and reviewers started to hold him to impossible standards, frequently ignoring his more avant-garde endeavors in favor of his popular songs. Some now viewed Depp's once-celebrated openness to take artistic chances as a weakness.

The Price of Disputation

Following several scandals that dogged his career, Depp's fame's darker side became more and more obvious. A man battling the burden of his fame was depicted by accusations of substance misuse, unpredictable conduct, and legal issues with past managers and ex-partners.

These conflicts had far-reaching effects. Depp lost lucrative gigs and endorsements, such as his famous performance in the *Pirates of the Caribbean* franchise as Captain Jack Sparrow. Once-competitive studios were reluctant to work with him, and media narratives frequently eclipsed his creative accomplishments.

Depp maintained his defiance in the face of these obstacles, adamantly claiming his innocence and battling to clear his name. Many of his admirers supported him during his public trials because of his ability to bounce back from setbacks.

Notoriety as a Two-Sided Blade

Despite all of the difficulties that fame has presented, Depp has also recognized how it has allowed him to pursue his artistic goals. His international fame gave him the chance to work with avant-garde filmmakers, play unusual parts, and pursue his love of music and the arts. He has, however, frequently voiced conflicting feelings about the perks of fame, characterizing it as both a boon and a bane.

Perhaps Depp's lasting popularity as a performer best captures his relationship with fame. His fans are incredibly loyal despite the scandals and losses because they are captivated by the unadulterated emotion and vulnerability he infuses into his work. This relationship highlights the paradox of fame: although it has the power to alienate and mislead, it also forges a connection between an artist and their audience that goes beyond the news.

Takeaways

Depp has learned to handle the challenges of celebrity with a combination of fortitude, humor, and self-reflection through the highs and lows of his career. He has frequently discussed the value of remaining loyal to oneself despite constant criticism. Depp believes that staying famous requires concentrating on his work and finding comfort in the people and interests that are most important to him.

A Warning Story

In an age of constant media attention and social media amplification, Johnny Depp's narrative serves as a potent reminder of the cost of celebrity. Although he has gained a position among Hollywood's elite due to his talent and charisma, the difficulties he has encountered underscore the human cost of being in the spotlight.

Depp's journey serves as a warning and an inspiration to fans and aspiring artists alike, illustrating the dangers and pleasures of living a life of dream-chasing under the spotlight. In the end, Depp's resilience and growth in the face of celebrity stress are testaments to his inner strength and persistent dedication to his art.

CHAPTER 5: THE WORDS OF JOHNNY DEPP

ON ACTING AND ART

Acting is more than just a job to Johnny Depp; it's a deep way for him to express himself, and art in all its forms is a haven for his imagination. Beyond the flimsy glamour of Hollywood success, Depp has embraced acting and art with a sense of purpose and passion throughout his life. Every character is a work of art in progress, every role is a canvas, and every creative project is a mirror of his spirit. His work has been shaped by this concept, which has also made him one of the most recognized and adaptable artists of his generation.

The Acting Philosophy

From the start of his career, Depp refused to follow the conventional route taken by Hollywood's top actors. He was an immediate heartthrob due to his attractiveness and early success on **21 Jump Street (1987–1991),** but he soon became disenchanted with the perks of celebrity and the cliched parts that accompanied it. Depp, on the other hand, looked for parts that pushed him, parts that let him play misfits, outsiders, and dreamers.

Acting is a very personal experience for Depp. He has frequently explained his method as completely engrossing himself in his characters' worlds and using his feelings and experiences to give them life. His representations of well-known characters like Sweeney Todd, Edward Scissorhands, and Captain Jack Sparrow from *Pirates of the Caribbean* demonstrate this commitment. Depp's performances have resonated with audiences of all ages because of his ability to portray these characters with complexity and realism.

Depp has discussed the inherent vulnerability of acting in interviews. He sees it as a chance to learn more about human nature and uncover truths about both the outside world and himself. "Acting," he once stated, "is about being as true as you can at the moment, but also finding freedom within that truth." His performances are so captivating because of this harmony between sincerity and originality.

A Passion for the Unusual

Depp's passion for the unusual and the extraordinary is evident in his career. From the darkly humorous Willy Wonka in **Charlie and the Chocolate Factory** to the fanciful Mad Hatter in **Alice in Wonderland**, he has consistently favored parts that let him push the envelope. Depp's reputation as an actor who isn't afraid to take chances and try new things has been further solidified by his partnerships with avant-garde filmmakers like Terry Gilliam, Gore Verbinski, and Tim Burton.

Depp's ability to bring emotion and depth to even the most fanciful characters is what makes him unique. For example, his portrayal of Captain Jack Sparrow used comedy, eccentricity, and vulnerability to redefine the swashbuckling hero paradigm. A one-dimensional part became a cultural phenomenon due to Depp's insistence on adding his eccentricities, such as emulating Sparrow's mannerisms after Rolling Stones guitarist Keith Richards.

Beyond the Screen: The Artist

Beyond acting, Depp pursues many other artistic endeavors. He is a talented musician who has played guitar in a number of bands and worked with legendary musicians like Jeff Beck, Joe Perry, and Alice Cooper. His passion for music precedes his acting career, and he frequently attributes his ability to bounce back from adversity to it. Depp views music as more than just a passion; it's a means of fostering relationships and conveying feelings that words cannot describe.

Another medium that Depp uses to express his ideas is visual art. His distinctive outlook on life is reflected in his paintings, which are frequently distinguished by their vivid hues and intense emotional content. With critically acclaimed shows and collections, Depp has started showcasing his artwork to the globe in recent years. He provides a window into his inner world by examining issues of identity, love, and grief in his artwork.

The Spirit of Collaboration

Depp's collaborative nature is another factor contributing to his success as an artist. He tackles every endeavor with humility and an open mind, whether collaborating with filmmakers, actors, or musicians. Depp, who sees the creative process as a journey rather than a solo undertaking, has frequently commended his collaborators for motivating him and pushing him to new heights.

An excellent illustration of this dynamic is his long-standing collaboration with Tim Burton. They have collaborated to create some of the most iconic movies of the last thirty years, including *Sleepy Hollow* and *Edward Scissorhands*. Although Burton has frequently referred to Depp as a kindred spirit who gives his characters unmatched depth, Depp attributes his freedom to try new things and take chances to Burton.

The Influence of Art

For Depp, art is a lifeline rather than merely a career. He has used acting, music, and painting as coping mechanisms and sources of comfort during some of the most trying times in his life. He may explore his identity, analyze his feelings, and establish a stronger connection with audiences through art.

According to Depp's reflections on his career, "Art should disturb the comfortable and comfort the disturbed." Whether he is creating a haunting song, portraying a misunderstood outcast, or painting a portrait that embodies the frailty of the human soul, this idea guides his work.

A Creative Legacy

As an artist, Johnny Depp's history is characterized by his willingness to take chances, his dedication to authenticity, and his capacity to elevate the commonplace to the extraordinary. His art enables viewers to view the world from a fresh perspective, questions norms and defies expectations.

In the end, Depp's development as an actor and artist serves as evidence of the transformational potential of art. He continues to be an unwavering supporter of originality and self-expression in a society that is frequently dominated by consumerism and uniformity, encouraging innumerable others to value their own distinctive voices. Depp's work never fails to enthrall, challenge, and endure whether it is displayed on canvas, stage, or screen.

ON LIFE AND FAME

A creative genius negotiating the demands of success, a highly introspective person battling the chaotic world around him, and an exceedingly private man forced into the blazing spotlight—Johnny Depp's life and career trajectory is an intriguing examination of contrasts. As he attempted to strike a balance between the demands of his work and his identity, Depp's life and fame have been intricately entwined and frequently in conflict with one another. Depp has developed a worldview that embodies fortitude, inventiveness, and a deep comprehension of human nature across it all.

A Life Philosopher

Depp has always had an inquisitive attitude to life. He was born in Owensboro, Kentucky, on June 9, 1963, and had a turbulent upbringing that included many transfers and his parents' eventual divorce. His perspective was formed by these early difficulties, which gave him a profound understanding of the brittleness and unpredictable nature of life. Depp's capacity to turn suffering into art became a recurrent theme in his life, inspiring him to pursue his artistic goals and supporting him through difficult times.

Depp has frequently discussed the value of leading a genuine life throughout the years. He believes that embracing uniqueness and upholding one's morals are more important in life than following social norms or striving for flimsy achievement. His personal and professional decisions reflect this mentality. He has always favored parts that defy expectations and provide a more profound understanding of the human condition, prioritizing sincerity over box office success.

The Sword of Fame with Two Edges

For Johnny Depp, fame arrived quickly and without warning. He became a teenage idol suddenly thanks to his breakthrough performance in **21 Jump Street**, but the rapid surge in popularity was both a boon and a bane. It put him under constant scrutiny even if it also led him to amazing possibilities. Depp soon discovered that being famous has a high cost, including the loss of privacy, the need to uphold a certain image, and the ongoing criticism from the public and media.

Depp's unease with celebrity was evident from a young age. He refused to be confined to the role of a traditional leading man, defying the Hollywood mold. Rather, he looked for oddball, outlandish personalities that let him show his uniqueness. By doing this, he established a distinct niche for himself, winning praise from critics and defying accepted conventions in celebrity society.

But the shadow of celebrity hung heavy. His artistic accomplishments were frequently eclipsed by the ongoing focus on his personal life, especially his romances and legal disputes. Every aspect of Depp's turbulent marriage to actress Amber Heard and the ensuing legal issues was publicly examined, turning it into a media circus. This intrusion into Depp's personal life served as a sad reminder of the less pleasant aspects of celebrity, which he has called "devastating" and "dehumanizing."

Using Creativity to Find Comfort

Creativity has always been Depp's remedy for the demands of celebrity. He has found comfort in artistic expression, whether it is through painting, acting, or singing. In particular, acting gives him a way to escape by letting him take on the roles of various individuals and discover fresh viewpoints. Depp has frequently compared acting to therapy as a means of expressing his feelings and understanding the world.

Depp also has a special place in his heart for music. He played guitar in a band before becoming an actor, and his passion for music hasn't lessened. Working with musicians like Alice Cooper and Jeff Beck has allowed Depp to express himself outside of the Hollywood bubble. For Depp, music is essentially a place of freedom where he can create without the demands of celebrity and reconnect with his roots.

Notoriety as an Instructor

Depp sees celebrity as a teaching tool despite its difficulties. He has learned perseverance, humility, and the value of surrounding oneself with sincere people as a result of it. Depp has gotten pickier over the years about who he lets into his inner group, giving preference to bonds based on respect and trust. Despite the chaos of his public life, his children, Lily-Rose and Jack, continue to be his greatest sources of inspiration and delight.

Depp also admits that his platform as an artist is boosted by his notoriety. It has enabled him to convey stories that connect with millions of people worldwide, reach a global audience, and leave a lasting impression through his work. Even though he might not live the life of a celebrity, he is aware of the opportunities that come with being famous and makes an effort to make the most of them.

Identity Reflections

Depp's thoughts on identity are among the most significant facets of his philosophy. He has frequently discussed the fluidity of identity and how life is a never-ending process of change. For Depp, being famous is not what defines him; it is only one aspect of who he is. He sees himself primarily as an artist, a storyteller dedicated to delving into the intricacies of the human condition.

Depp's self-examination also encompasses his conception of success. Depp gauges success by the influence of his work and the relationships he forms with people, whereas many people associate success with money and honors. He is proud of his capacity to upend conventions, excite audiences, and leave a legacy of originality and sincerity.

A Legacy That Goes Beyond Stardom

Johnny Depp's attitude toward life and celebrity is evidence of his fortitude and creative ability. Using his experiences to inspire his creativity and mold his perspective, he has purposefully navigated the highs and lows of stardom. According to Depp, life is about finding purpose in hardships, transforming them into art, and remaining loyal to oneself rather than escaping them.

As an artist, Depp's creations speak to viewers on a very human level, beyond the boundaries of celebrity. Through his well-known concerts, songs, and paintings, he never stops encouraging others to value their uniqueness and see the beauty in their flaws.

In the end, Depp's thoughts on life and celebrity show a guy who is both grounded and reflective, a creative spirit resolved to live true to himself in a society that frequently expects conformity. His story is a potent reminder that a person's capacity to stay true to themselves in the face of popularity is a more accurate indicator of their character than their level of recognition.

QUOTES TO INSPIRE

More than just an actor, Johnny Depp is a thinker and artist whose words frequently strike a profound chord with his followers and lovers. His speeches, interviews, and informal discussions throughout the years have shown him to be a deeply reflective and perceptive individual. The quotations by Depp provide insight into his views on fame, individualism, art, and life and can be a source of motivation for people attempting to forge their paths. His reputation as a voice of innovation and wisdom has been solidified by his ability to convey difficult feelings and concepts in straightforward yet powerful language.

About Individuality and Authenticity

The value of remaining true to oneself is among Johnny Depp's most persistent themes. Depp has continuously defended originality as a means of achieving contentment and happiness, having experienced the pressures of conformity from a young age. He once stated, * "There's a drive in me that won't allow me to do certain things that are easy." * This remark captures his reluctance to follow the easy path in both his personal and professional life, choosing instead to make decisions that align with his true personality.

Depp famously said, **"It's only a bad day, not a bad life." He has also urged others to embrace their individuality**. These succinct but impactful words serve as a reminder that hardships and disappointments are transitory and that tenacity can bring about better times. Numerous admirers have been motivated to accept their imperfections and maintain optimism throughout trying times by their capacity to find beauty in imperfection and strength in adversity.

His philosophy is encapsulated in the following quote: **"Laugh as much as you breathe and love as long as you live."** Depp's conviction in the value of interpersonal relationships and emotional health is further supported by this moving admonition to put joy and love above financial achievement.

About Art and Creativity

For Johnny Depp, being an artist is a way of life rather than just a career. His thoughts on creativity demonstrate his profound understanding of the transformational potential of artistic expression. "Music touches us emotionally, where words alone can't," he once remarked. The immense effect that music—and, by extension, all kinds of art—can have on the human soul is highlighted in this quotation.

Another comment from Depp that demonstrates his commitment to his work is **"You can close your eyes to the things you don't want to see, but you can't close your heart to the things you don't want to feel."** His approach to acting, in which he digs deeply into his emotions to give his characters authenticity, is reflected in this insightful comment. It also acts as a reminder that honesty and vulnerability are important to creativity in its purest form.

On Notoriety and Its Difficulties

Having been in the public eye for decades, Depp has a complex view of celebrity. He has been outspoken about its negative features while still acknowledging its positive qualities. **"People say I make strange choices, but they're not strange for me,"** he said in one interview. **My illness stems from my fascination with human nature, human behavior, and the inner worlds of people.** This declaration demonstrates his determination to investigate the intricacies of the human condition despite criticism from the general public.

Depp frequently expresses his desire for privacy and simplicity in his thoughts on celebrity. **"Fame is a beast," he once observed. Additionally, it will eat everything in its way.** This striking insight is a warning to people who pursue popularity without considering the repercussions, as well as a critique of celebrity culture.

Regarding Love and Life

Johnny Depp is fundamentally a romantic and a philosopher who sees significance in the little things in life. **"The only creatures that are evolved enough to convey pure love are dogs and infants."** is one of his most frequently cited statements. His conviction in the purity of unconditional love is emphasized by this poignant yet hilarious speech, which strikes a deep chord with his supporters.

Depp has equally profound ideas about love. He once stated, **"Love is not blind; it simply enables one to see things others fail to see**." The transformational power of love is encapsulated in this poetic contemplation, which also emphasizes how it may help us better comprehend both ourselves and other people.

On Hope and Perseverance

Depp's career has been full of highs and lows, and his words show how resilient he has been in the face of hardship. His words, **"Keep going forward,"** are among his most motivational quotes. Keep going. **Continue regardless of what occurs.** Many people have been inspired by these words to persevere through difficulties and never give up on their goals, no matter how impossible they may appear.

"The problem is not the problem" is another potent quotation. Your perspective on the issue is the issue. This nugget of wisdom promotes a change of viewpoint by serving as a reminder that our approach to challenges frequently dictates the result.

Leave a Legacy With Words

People from various walks of life can find inspiration and wisdom in Johnny Depp's statements, which go beyond his job as an actor and artist. His thoughts are universally relatable, whether they are about the difficulties of celebrity, the pleasures of love, or the significance of remaining true to oneself.

In the end, these quotations capture the spirit of Johnny Depp, a man who has led a complex, imaginative, and genuine life. In addition to being a well-liked musician, he is also a source of inspiration and wisdom for millions of people worldwide because of his ability to communicate difficult realities in a way that is relevant. Depp's comments continue to encourage us to value our uniqueness, follow our passions, and see the beauty in life's flaws.

CHAPTER 6: BEYOND THE SILVER SCREEN – ENTREPRENEUR AND PHILANTHROPIST

ENTREPRENEURIAL VENTURES

The impact of Johnny Depp goes much beyond the movie industry. Although he is regarded as one of the most adaptable actors of his time, his business endeavors show a more lively side to him. Depp has pursued a variety of commercial ventures throughout the years, showcasing his inventiveness, daring nature, and commitment to artistic expression. Depp's business ventures, which range from starting his own production company to working with others on distinctive projects in the fields of fashion, music, and wine, highlight his diverse skill set and dedication to leaving a legacy that goes beyond his acting career.

Building Creative Foundations: Infinitum Nihil

Infinitum Nihil, which translates to "Nothing is Forever" in Latin, is the production business that Johnny Depp founded in 2004. Depp's ambition to take charge of his creative path gave rise to the business, which enabled him to deliver tales that mainstream Hollywood might otherwise ignore. Among the highly regarded films that Infinitum Nihil has produced are **The Rum Diary (2011), Hugo (2011), and Minamata (2020).**

From choosing screenplays to forming the artistic vision of his movies, Depp's involvement in the filming process is evident in his job as a producer. Depp has promoted autonomous storytelling via Infinitum Nihil, frequently emphasizing original plots and underdog characters that suit his aesthetic preferences. His legacy as a producer who values content over spectacle has been cemented by his dedication to quality and uniqueness, which has helped bring intricate, unusual stories to audiences throughout the world.

Musical Adventures

Johnny Depp's love of music precedes his acting career, and he has skillfully integrated it into his business endeavors. Depp is a talented guitarist who has worked with some of the biggest names in music. He joined Alice Cooper and Joe Perry of Aerosmith to form the rock band Hollywood Vampires in 2015. The group showcases Depp's musical abilities while also paying homage to the rock icons of the past.

Depp's commitment to music as a genuine endeavor rather than a side activity is demonstrated by Hollywood Vampires' several record releases and international tours. His band's branding, live performances, and collaborations all reflect his entrepreneurial mentality, which has helped the band establish a solid name in the rock music industry. Depp's collaboration with Hollywood Vampires is a prime example of how he can combine his love of art with business savvy to produce a project that is both artistically rewarding and financially profitable.

The Sauvage Collaboration

One of Depp's most well-known forays into the fashion and beauty industries was his role as the face of Dior's *Sauvage* fragrance in 2015. His partnership with Dior has been a huge success, and the campaign has grown to become one of the most iconic and long-lasting in the luxury advertising industry. Depp's tough charm and mysterious demeanor perfectly capture the essence of *Sauvage*, which contributed to the fragrance's success as a worldwide bestseller.

This collaboration demonstrates Depp's impact as a cultural figure and his capacity to enhance a brand via his affiliation. In addition to the campaign's financial success, Depp's participation has strengthened his standing as a style icon and a person who goes beyond the conventional bounds of celebrity.

Châte de Depp: Winemaking

During his years in France, Depp's passion for good wine inspired him to pursue a winemaking career. Although he hasn't officially started his wine label, Depp restored the grapes on his expansive Provence estate and made wine for his own consumption and limited distribution. Since he sees winemaking as both an art form and a way to connect with the land, Depp's profound admiration for the craft is consistent with his artistic worldview.

Even though Depp's winemaking endeavors are quite discreet, they demonstrate his love of fine craftsmanship and his wish to pursue artistic endeavors outside of the entertainment sector.

Collaborations in the Arts

Depp has also embraced visual art as a means of enterprise and self-expression in recent years. His paintings, which are frequently distinguished by their rich hues and profound emotional content, have been exhibited and offered for sale as limited-edition prints. Themes of identity, celebrity, and resiliency are central to Depp's artwork, which appeals to both fans and collectors.

His entry into the art industry demonstrates his spirit of entrepreneurship and his capacity to turn a personal interest into a profitable economic venture. In addition to receiving praise from critics, Depp's artwork has given him a fresh and personal method to interact with viewers, thus extending his creative legacy.

Entrepreneurial Philanthropy

Depp's business endeavors also include philanthropy, where he uses his business sense to promote worthy causes. He has participated in fundraising campaigns for cancer research, children's hospitals, and disaster relief, frequently leveraging his celebrity to increase the impact of these causes. According to Depp, being an entrepreneur is about changing the world for the better as well as making money.

His generosity to the Great Ormond Street Hospital in London, where he has contributed the money he makes from his business endeavors and even paid unexpected visits in the guise of Captain Jack Sparrow to cheer up young patients, is one noteworthy example. Depp's belief in the value of giving back and using his position for good is reflected in this fusion of business and philanthropy.

Keeping Business and Passion in Balance

Depp's ability to strike a balance between enthusiasm and financial acumen is demonstrated by his entrepreneurial endeavors. Depp pursues every project with the same commitment and sincerity that characterize his acting profession, whether it be producing movies, working with musicians, or making art. In addition to building his brand, he pursues endeavors that are consistent with his artistic vision and principles.

Depp's business endeavors are notable for their authenticity and uniqueness in a world where celebrity entrepreneurship frequently seems artificial. He has demonstrated that genuine entrepreneurship involves more than just making money; it also entails making significant and enduring contributions to society.

A Creative Heritage

Like his acting career, Johnny Depp's entrepreneurial path is unique and varied. From the movie theater to the recording studio, from French vineyards to international art galleries, Depp's endeavors demonstrate his unbridled inventiveness and his refusal to be constrained by preconceived notions. In addition to broadening his creative horizons, Depp's business endeavors have cemented his status as a cultural icon whose influence goes well beyond Hollywood.

Depp's impact as an entrepreneur ultimately reflects his artistic philosophy, which is to question norms, take chances, and produce work that speaks to the heart and soul. His endeavors are an ode to uniqueness, zeal, and the timeless potential of creativity.

GIVING BACK

Although Johnny Depp is renowned throughout the world for his extraordinary acting ability, his charitable endeavors, and deeds of kindness also show a very caring side that frequently functions behind the scenes. Depp's dedication to charitable giving goes beyond simply writing checks or endorsing charities; it is based on a sincere desire to change the world, deeply personal connections, and empathy. His humanitarian activities have covered a wide range of topics throughout the years, from disaster relief to healthcare, from empowering marginalized people to promoting the arts.

A Child's Health Advocate

Johnny Depp's devotion to children's hospitals is among his most sincere pledges. Due to his daughter Lily-Rose's previous hospitalization for a serious illness, he has a very personal connection to this cause. Depp was forever changed by the experience, which motivated him to support the organizations that had given his family hope.

Depp has frequently opted to donate anonymously to children's hospitals around the world. In addition to financial support, he has visited numerous young patients in the persona of Captain Jack Sparrow, bringing them joy. In medical wards, Depp has spent hours conversing with youngsters, telling stories, and making people laugh while wearing full pirate gear. Parents and hospital employees have characterized these visits as life-changing experiences that lift the children's and their families' moods.

His long-standing partnership with Great Ormond Street Hospital in London, where he generously gave a sizeable amount of his *Pirates of the Caribbean* profits, is one noteworthy example. More children now have access to life-saving medicines thanks to his deeds of generosity, which have also improved facilities and funded vital medical research.

Promote the Arts

Johnny Depp has continuously backed programs that encourage the arts and provide young people with opportunities because he is an artist who cherishes creativity in all its manifestations. In order to bring the transforming power of art to underprivileged communities, he has worked with organizations, financed scholarships for young actors and filmmakers, and contributed to arts education programs.

Depp's attempts to keep music instruction in schools alive have been inspired by his love of music in particular. He has supported music programs, donated instruments, and taken part in benefit performances to spread the word about the value of art education because he understands how important music is for encouraging creativity and emotional expression.

Depp and his band, the Hollywood Vampires, co-founded the yearly *Raise the Dead* fundraiser performance series in 2012. In order to provide the future generation with the resources and motivation they need to follow their aspirations, the proceeds from these events are donated to charities that assist young musicians, music therapy programs, and other creative endeavors.

Global Causes and Disaster Relief

Disaster relief activities have also been a part of Depp's philanthropy. Depp has continuously stepped up in times of need, whether it is helping victims of natural disasters like hurricanes and earthquakes or supporting international humanitarian initiatives. He has collaborated with groups like UNICEF and the Red Cross to help people in need, frequently using his notoriety to raise awareness of pressing problems.

He made a significant contribution to relief operations after the 2010 Haitian earthquake, which proved devastating. In addition to participating in campaigns to increase awareness of the Haitian people's ongoing recovery needs, Depp gave a substantial donation. His actions demonstrate his readiness to use his position to assist marginalized groups globally.

Environmental Advocacy and Animal Welfare

Depp has made major contributions to animal welfare organizations as a result of his well-documented love of animals. Depp has demonstrated a strong devotion to animal welfare by supporting the preservation of endangered species and making donations to shelters and rescue organizations.

His support of programs that fight deforestation, protect marine ecosystems, and address climate change is only one example of how his environmental involvement demonstrates his compassion. Working with groups like Conservation International and Greenpeace, Depp has contributed his voice to campaigns highlighting the significance of preserving the environment for coming generations.

Individual Generosities

Johnny Depp is well-known for his private deeds of kindness in addition to his public charitable endeavors. Many of these tales are revealed by the testimonies of those he has assisted rather than by press releases. Depp has subtly changed the lives of many by assisting strangers in need and paying for friends' and coworkers' medical bills.

The making of **Pirates of the Caribbean** is a well-known instance of his generosity. According to a staff worker, Depp made sure everyone was comfortable despite the extreme weather by purchasing coats for the whole crew during a particularly chilly shot. In a similar vein, he frequently goes above and above to show appreciation and goodwill by surprising fans and staff with well-considered gifts.

Compassion Legacy

Johnny Depp's charitable endeavors demonstrate his conviction in the value of giving back and the efficacy of kindness. His deeds, whether they be large-scale or small-scale acts of kindness, reveal a profound awareness of the positive effects that compassion can have on people and societies.

Depp's genuineness is the foundation of his charitable legacy. Depp's donations are motivated by a sincere desire to help people in need and empathy, in contrast to many celebrities who view charity as a branding exercise. Depp has continuously used his riches and influence to improve the world, whether it is by helping emerging artists, helping sick children, or supporting international relief efforts.

Ultimately, Johnny Depp's dedication to charitable work is just as essential to who he is as his creative accomplishments. His deeds serve as a reminder that genuine greatness comes from having the capacity to raise people, inspire hope, and make a positive impact on the world in addition to having skill and accomplishment. Depp's impact goes well beyond the entertainment industry thanks to his philanthropy, which further exemplifies the virtues of kindness, generosity, and humanity.

A CREATIVE LEGACY

Johnny Depp is a cultural figure whose influence cuts across decades thanks to his contributions to the fields of music, art, film, and philanthropy. Millions of people around the world have been inspired by Depp's creative legacy, which extends beyond his renowned acting career and includes bold innovation, artistic integrity, and a dedication to authenticity. Depp is now more than simply a Hollywood star; he is a representation of uniqueness and artistic bravery thanks to his legacy, which has been molded by decades of life-changing performances and an uncompromising commitment to artistic expression.

Reviving the Acting Craft

Depp's innovative acting career lies at the core of his artistic heritage. Depp has shown a readiness to take chances and accept unusual parts since the beginning of his career. Whether playing quirky characters like Captain Jack Sparrow or Edward Scissorhands or assuming profoundly reflective parts in movies like **Finding Neverland,** Depp added a degree of complexity and delicacy that went against conventional ideas of Hollywood celebrity.

Depp's ability to blend in with his characters was what made him unique. He was able to create characters that were both memorable and complicated because of his systematic approach and natural sensitivity. For instance, Depp's performance as Captain Jack Sparrow not only revolutionized the pirate genre but also established himself as a cultural icon, securing him a nomination for an Academy Award and a permanent position in popular culture.

A generation of performers has been impacted by Depp's dedication to being honest in his characters. His ability to strike a balance between artistic integrity and popular popularity serves as a model for performers who want to contribute significantly to their craft.

A Passion for Music Throughout Life

Johnny Depp had aspirations of becoming a musician long before he became an actor. This enthusiasm never wavered, and Depp skillfully combined his love of music with his artistic endeavors throughout his life. As a guitarist and one of the founding members of the rock band Hollywood Vampires, Depp has proven that his abilities are not limited to the movie industry.

Depp has honored the rock icons that influenced him with Hollywood Vampires while simultaneously releasing fresh music that appeals to listeners. Both fans and seasoned musicians revere him for his performances, which are distinguished by their technical mastery and unadulterated emotion. Depp's work in this field has encouraged many aspiring artists to pursue their goals, and his musical legacy is proof of his conviction that creativity has no bounds.

Encouraging the Craft of Narration

Another aspect of Depp's legacy is his capacity to support marginalized and distinctive narratives. Depp has played a key role in bringing unorthodox stories to reality through his production business, Infinitum Nihil. His commitment to examining issues of justice, resiliency, and the human condition is evident in films such as *Minamata* and *The Rum Diary*.

Depp's determination to make pictures with depth and substance has caused a stir in an industry that is sometimes dominated by economic concerns. Independent filmmakers and storytellers who might not have otherwise had a venue for their voices have benefited from his efforts.

An Artist of the Renaissance

Acting and music are not the only aspects of Depp's legacy. He has adopted visual art as an additional means of self-expression in recent years. His paintings provide insight into the inner workings of his creative mind because of their vivid hues and intensely intimate themes. Fans and collectors alike find resonance in Depp's artwork, which ranges from abstract explorations of identity and fame to portraits of cultural icons.

His entry into the art scene further solidifies his reputation as a contemporary Renaissance man—someone who sees the quest of creation as an endless endeavor. Regardless matter their medium or experience, others have been motivated to explore their own creative potential by Depp's artistic pursuits.

Philanthropic Inspiration

Depp's dedication to giving back is a part of his creative legacy. His charitable endeavors, which range from disaster relief to children's hospitals, demonstrate his faith in the transformational potential of generosity and goodwill. Depp's legacy has been further amplified by his activities, which have motivated peers and fans alike to use their platforms for good.

For instance, his charity visits to children's hospitals while posing as Captain Jack Sparrow have become famous. These scenes demonstrate how Depp's inventiveness transcends the screen and gives people in need happiness and hope.

The Icon of Culture Who Disregarded Tradition

Depp's capacity to subvert expectations and reinterpret what it means to be a star also defines his creative legacy. He has always blazed his trail as an artist and a person, never fitting in with Hollywood's norms. He has become a cultural figure whose influence extends well beyond the entertainment sector thanks to his distinctive fusion of charisma, vulnerability, and artistic bravery.

Depp has had a lasting impact on contemporary culture, from establishing new benchmarks for character-driven narratives to influencing fashion trends. Both the lasting appeal of the characters and universes he has contributed to, as well as the innumerable actors, musicians, and artists who credit him with influencing them, are testaments to his influence.

A Durable Legacy

Resilience, genuineness, and an unrelenting dedication to art in all its manifestations characterize Johnny Depp's artistic history. His career serves as a tribute to the strength of remaining loyal to oneself despite obstacles and criticism. Depp's status as one of the most significant personalities of his generation has been cemented by his ability to turn personal hardships into gripping performances and significant social achievements.

New generations of artists and visionaries will continue to be inspired by Depp's work as the years go by. His legacy serves as a reminder that being creative involves more than just creating outstanding art; it also entails questioning conventions, forming relationships, and making a significant and enduring contribution to society. Although Johnny Depp's career is far from complete, he has already cemented his position in the annals of art, culture, and mankind.

CHAPTER 7: THE RECENT YEARS – TRIALS, TRIUMPHS, AND REINVENTION

LEGAL BATTLES AND PUBLIC REDEMPTION

Off-screen, Johnny Depp's life has been characterized by well-publicized legal disputes and personal hardships, many of which have dominated news reports for years. Even though they were challenging, these obstacles helped him become resilient and eventually find public redemption. In addition to being some of the most carefully watched celebrity court cases of the twenty-first century, Depp's legal troubles—especially his turbulent relationship with ex-wife Amber Heard—also highlight his nuanced relationship with notoriety, reputation, and personal development.

The Claims of Domestic Abuse and Divorce

Actress Amber Heard and Johnny Depp's marriage ended abruptly and in the public eye in 2016. Both parties made harsh accusations during their divorce, but Heard's charges of domestic violence were what put Depp in the spotlight. A contentious and emotional legal battle resulted from Heard's accusations that Depp had physically abused him during their relationship. Depp, however, strongly refuted the charges, asserting that he had been subjected to both physical and emotional assault.

As the public trial unfolded in real-time across news sources, social media, and tabloids, the claims marked a turning point in Depp's career. As Heard was portrayed as a victim and Depp as a villain by the media, Depp's status as a cherished Hollywood icon rapidly changed. Depp's career suffered a great deal as a result of the controversy, and he was fired from several big movie franchises, including the *Fantastic Beasts* and *Pirates of the Caribbean* franchises.

Depp insisted that he was innocent despite the increased scrutiny and media hysteria surrounding the issue, claiming that Heard had launched a smear campaign against him. As the consequences of the accusations spread, Depp's career suffered significant blows in a field that sometimes puts public opinion ahead of the facts.

Counterclaims and Defamation Lawsuits

Even though the divorce settlement was reached in 2017, Depp and Heard's legal disputes grew more intense over the ensuing years. After Heard penned an opinion piece for *The Washington Post* in which she identified herself as a victim of domestic abuse, Depp sued her for $50 million in defamation in 2018. Depp claimed that even though the piece did not specifically name him, it inferred that he was the abuser, which hurt his career and reputation. The goal of the case was to restore his reputation and clear his name.

Heard responded by filing a $100 million countersuit, alleging that Depp's attorneys had defamed her by referring to her charges as a fake. Both parties gave their versions of events in court, making the defamation lawsuits a drawn-out and challenging process. For years, the cases continued to drag on, with every discovery stoking the flames.

Heard's attorneys insisted that Depp had been violent and abusive during their marriage, while Depp's side portrayed Heard as a cunning and manipulative person. The media persisted in sensationalizing the matter, and both sides were under great public scrutiny.

The "Sun" Newspaper and the UK Libel Case

Apart from the legal actions brought against Heard, Depp was also involved in a well-known libel case in the UK. After the British tabloid **The Sun** called him a **"wife-beater"** in an article about his marriage to Heard, Depp filed a libel suit against the publication and its publisher, News Group Newspapers, in 2018. When the court decided in favor of **The Sun**, the case drastically changed from Depp's attempt to clear his name.

Citing proof that Depp had physically abused Heard several times throughout their relationship, the court determined that the publication's allegations were "substantially true." The ruling severely harmed Depp's reputation and dealt a serious blow to his legal strategy. Depp faced a formidable uphill struggle in his quest for atonement after the UK case ended in a defeat since the decision appeared to validate the abuse claims brought against him.

A Watershed Moment and the Virginia Trial

Depp's defamation claim against Heard in Virginia was a significant turning point, notwithstanding the failures in the UK libel case. With its intense courtroom discussions and scandalous details, the trial, which started in 2022, enthralled spectators around the world. Depp had the chance to take on the accusations directly and restore his reputation in a court of law with this litigation.

Depp's defense team put up a fierce fight during the trial, trying to show that Heard's allegations were not only untrue but also a part of a calculated effort to harm Depp's reputation. In his moving and intensely personal testimony, Depp gave his version of events and discussed the emotional and psychological toll the public charges had placed on him. To refute Heard's account of what happened, his defense team also produced documents, witness accounts, and audio recordings that called into question her veracity.

The public's perception started to change in favor of Depp as the trial went on. Once vehemently critical of him, public opinion began to shift in favor of Depp, with many fans and onlookers voicing their support. As Depp battled to restore his honor and reputation, the trial came to represent his redemption. By the time the jury found in Depp's favor in 2022, the case had come to represent the larger cultural discussion surrounding abuse, celebrity, and the influence of the media.

How the Trials Affected Depp's Image

Depp's work and personal life have been significantly impacted by the court fights and defamation cases. His accomplishments were eclipsed for years by the abuse allegations, and he was cut off from many members of the Hollywood elite due to the media hysteria surrounding his divorce and legal actions. However, Depp was able to start the process of repairing his reputation because he resolved to clear his name and his eventual win in the Virginia trial.

Even while Depp's legal triumphs did not instantly result in a full return to the glory of his former career, viewers who had followed the trials started to find resonance in his story of redemption. The public's view of Depp changed from one of a man who had been manipulated by the media to one who had suffered severe losses in both his personal and professional life but had come out of the shadows with largely intact integrity.

The Path to Salvation

Even though Depp's path through court cases and public atonement has been difficult and occasionally degrading, it has also shown his tenacity and capacity to endure in the face of insurmountable obstacles. Although it's still uncertain how his career will develop, Depp has been able to regain his place in the cultural discourse thanks to the defamation cases, court rulings, and the subsequent public shift in his favor.

But one thing is for sure: Depp's story is one of optimism and regeneration. Many have been inspired by his resolve to stand up for the truth and regain his dignity despite the years of turmoil. His legal struggles were about more than just clearing his name; they were about defending himself and not allowing lies to define his legacy. It is unclear how Depp's public atonement will affect his future as he navigates his post-trial life, but his experience serves as a reminder of the difficulties of celebrity, the price of controversy, and the strength of individual tenacity.

CAREER RESURGENCE

Both remarkable achievements and severe personal adversity have characterized Johnny Depp's career. His legal and personal struggles appeared to be about to put a stop to his career for a while. But Depp's comeback, which started in the middle of the 2020s, has been nothing short of extraordinary. Depp's career has started to find its footing, reminding audiences and the industry of his enormous talent and star power, thanks to his tenacity, the changing tides of public opinion, and several wise professional decisions.

Repair of the Image

Following years of being involved in legal and public disputes, Johnny Depp's reputation was severely damaged. Depp had fallen from grace in the film world due to allegations of abuse and his negative depiction in the media. His long-standing career appeared to be in danger, and major studios distanced themselves from him. However, Depp's loyal fan base and the support of his inner circle remained unwavering even during the darkest days.

Depp's well-publicized court triumph in the defamation action against Amber Heard in 2022 marked a sea change in his life. In addition to clearing his record of the abuse charges that had dogged him, this trial served as a cathartic outlet for Depp, enabling him to publicly face his accuser. Many people who had previously accepted the charges against him were reshaped by his heartfelt testimony, his candor, and his fortitude during the trial. This triumph demonstrated that Depp was still able to influence the industry and that the harm to his career might not be as severe as initially believed.

Even if his legal issues may have momentarily stopped his career's progress, Depp's comeback to the public eye signaled the start of a much-needed comeback. The favorable change in public opinion, particularly among his supporters, allowed Depp to prepare for a comeback by looking for parts that would both repair his reputation and utilize his enormous talent pool.

Independent Films' Function

113

Depp consciously decided to move toward more independent films in the years after his legal fights ended. After establishing his career with popular hits and blockbusters, Depp looked to independent film, where he could play more demanding, complex, and bold characters. By making this change, he was able to break out from the "Hollywood" image that had come to be connected with his previous scandals and concentrate on roles that showcased his full range as an actor.

Depp's portrayal of real-life photojournalist W. Eugene Smith in **Minamata (2020)** was one of the first movies that signaled his comeback. Smith's expose of the mercury poisoning by a Japanese chemical corporation, a cause Depp fervently supported, was the subject of the movie. Even in a more subdued, serious role, Depp's portrayal of Smith, a man struggling with the psychological and physical ramifications of his job, served as a reminder of his natural ability to evoke nuance and complexity. Depp's performance was praised for its emotional depth and honesty, and *Minamata* was a critical success. Even while the movie did not have a huge box office impact, it restored Depp's reputation as an actor who isn't afraid to take chances and breathe fresh life into compelling, real-life tales.

After this, Depp kept looking for parts in indie films that would let him experiment with different artistic mediums. Movies like **City of Lies** (2018) and **Waiting for the Barbarians (2019)** further showed Depp's dedication to tackling more somber, thought-provoking material, indicating that his skills had not waned despite years of turmoil. Working with directors who respected his talent and understood that Depp's character as an actor remained intact, Depp gradually started to restore his reputation through his independent cinema endeavors.

Iconic Roles Returning

Rumors of Depp rejoining big series started to surface as his career started to settle. Whether he will return to the character of Captain Jack Sparrow in the **Pirates of the Caribbean** franchise was perhaps the most anticipated question. Despite the difficulties that had surrounded him, many believed that Depp's portrayal of one of the most adored characters in contemporary film was not yet complete.

The public's lasting love for the character prompted discussions regarding Depp's comeback, even though the *Pirates* franchise had essentially moved on from his role following *Pirates of the Caribbean: Dead Men Tell No Tales* (2017). According to sources as of 2023, Depp was amenable to returning to the part in some manner, hoping for a new **Pirates** film that would let him play the swashbuckling role that had characterized a large portion of his career.

Even though Depp's return to **Pirates** hasn't happened yet, the prospect of Captain Jack returning is still a major factor in Depp's career comeback. For Depp as an actor and for the adored figure who, for many, came to be associated with his name, it is a kind of atonement. Depp's legacy is far from ended, as his comeback to big Hollywood franchises will surely culminate if he can return to the world of **Pirates**.

Partnerships with Prominent Directors

Resuming work with some of Hollywood's most prestigious filmmakers has been a major component of Depp's professional comeback. One of Depp's most enduring and successful working relationships was with filmmaker Tim Burton, who is considered to have one of the most recognizable director-actor pairs in contemporary filmmaking. Having collaborated on movies like *Edward Scissorhands*, *Sweeney Todd: The Demon Barber of Fleet Street*, and

Alice in Wonderland, Burton and Depp's distinct creative chemistry has produced some of Depp's most iconic roles.

Fans hoped that Burton would give Depp another important role in the years after his court troubles. When Depp and Burton announced in 2022 that they were collaborating on a new project, people became excited because they thought this would be the beginning of a new phase in Depp's artistic development. Burton's dark, whimsical aesthetic has always complemented Depp's ability to play complex, quirky characters, and a new movie in this collaboration would be the ideal chance for Depp to demonstrate his transformational skills on screen once more.

Depp is also once again being accepted into Hollywood's creative elite, as evidenced by his collaborations with other well-known filmmakers. He is a great asset to filmmakers looking for an actor with both star power and depth because of his dedication to his work, his unwavering love for performing, and his revitalized public persona.

A Novel Phase of Ingenuity

Johnny Depp's professional comeback involves more than just going back to his previous parts; it also involves accepting new challenges and pushing himself in previously unheard-of ways. Depp has demonstrated that his best work may still be in store for him with a renewed emphasis on independent film, partnerships with renowned filmmakers, and the prospect of returning to his famous roles.

For Depp, the past several years have been a time of significant transformation. His legacy will not be characterized by scandal or controversy because of his capacity to withstand the storm of public and legal upheaval and his unwavering dedication to his profession. In addition to being a win for Depp as an actor, his comeback is also a win for those who supported him during his most difficult times. His tale is proof of the enduring strength of skill, fortitude, and the capacity to begin again despite setbacks.

A NEW CHAPTER

Dramatic highs, heartbreaking lows, and the kind of public scrutiny that few celebrities ever encounter have all been part of Johnny Depp's life and career. However, Depp appears to be embarking on a new stage in both his personal and professional life as he comes out of the shadows cast by his widely reported legal and personal conflicts. Growth, reinvention, and the prospect of a future in which Depp can reshape his legacy according to his wishes characterize this new chapter.

Taking Advantage of New Possibilities

Johnny Depp's readiness to seize new chances that align with his developing creative vision is among the most important elements of his new chapter. Depp is returning to his craft with newfound vigor after years of negotiating turbulent seas in both his personal and professional lives. He is selecting projects that demonstrate his maturity and depth as an artist. This new stage appears to be more about pursuing jobs that speak to him personally than it is about chasing the celebrity and wealth that once characterized his career.

Depp's return to independent filmmaking has been a defining feature of his Hollywood comeback, but he has also demonstrated an openness to collaborating with up-and-coming artists and trying out new genres. These decisions represent a move away from the popular parts that made him famous and toward endeavors that let him express his creativity. This change, in many respects, represents Depp's evolution from a Hollywood star caught in the spotlight to a more sober, introspective artist looking for authentic expression.

Depp's drive for creative independence is now reflected in his employment choices. His dedication to presenting meaningful stories is demonstrated by his choice to focus on smaller, more personal projects, such as the 2020 movie *Minamata*. Depp shows that his artistic path is no longer determined by financial success but rather by a sincere desire to add to the cultural dialogue by embracing roles that center on complex human experiences and significant social issues. Because of this, his most recent work is marked by emotional resonance, depth, and vulnerability—elements that have become essential to his artistic identity in this new phase.

A Change in Public Attitude

The drama surrounding Depp's personal life, especially the widely reported legal disputes with his ex-wife, Amber Heard, damaged his reputation for many years. His career was marred by these scandals for a long time, and many people questioned if he would ever be able to return to his previous standing as one of Hollywood's most adored actors. But Depp's career took a significant turn in 2022 after he won his defamation lawsuit against Heard and the public began to sympathize with his version of events.

Millions of people across the world watched the 2022 trial, which turned out to be crucial to his career comeback in addition to serving as a moment of personal vindication. It was evident that public opinion was starting to change in Depp's favor as he won the slander action. With this win, Depp was able to take back his story, and the public's opinion of him started to change. In contrast to his previous reputation as a scandal-plagued figure, he was now widely perceived as a man who had stood up for what he believed in, suffered greatly, and come out stronger than before.

This change in perspective is intrinsically tied to Depp's new phase. He may never be able to completely shake the shadow of his previous scandals, but he now has the opportunity to be viewed in a way that acknowledges his genius, his tenacity, and his capacity to overcome hardship. In addition to giving Depp a platform to take on more varied parts and projects that demonstrate his artistic maturity, this shift in public opinion has allowed him to reenter the entertainment world with a revitalized sense of purpose and confidence.

Reinvention and Personal Development

Johnny Depp's personal development and reinvention are also important aspects of his new chapter. Depp has had severe personal hardships throughout the years, including turbulent relationships and his well-known drug addiction. However, Depp seems to be on a journey of introspection, recovery, and development as he comes out of the most trying time in his life. His latest public remarks and interviews show a man who has reflected on his previous transgressions and is dedicated to growing as a person and an artist.

Depp's oddities, love of portraying complicated, frequently disturbed characters, and dedication to living life on his terms have long been well-known. However, as he proceeds, a feeling of serenity and maturity appears to define this new phase. He is adopting a more grounded approach to both his personal and professional lives, as seen by his candid remarks about his wish to achieve balance in his life and to prioritize his well-being.

This time of introspection is about more than simply mending old scars; it's also about discovering new aspects of who he is. Depp is no longer merely defined by his previous roles or public persona, as evidenced by his continued involvement in music, his interest in painting, and his ambition to produce art that speaks to his inner reality. Instead, he is searching for true and satisfying ways to express himself while also utilizing the full extent of his creative ability.

A Comeback to Legendary Parts and Novel Projects

Depp is beginning to consider the notion of returning to some of the famous parts that first made him a star, even if his current career has been defined by his focus on smaller, more meaningful ventures. A sense of closure and resonance with the work that shaped his early career are signified by this return to familiar territory, especially the potential to reprise his role as Captain Jack Sparrow in the **Pirates of the Caribbean** franchise.

But Depp isn't only focusing on the past. He is constantly looking for new endeavors that represent his evolving artistic style and shifting interests. A major turning point in his career was his participation in the production of *La Favorite*, a

French historical drama in which he plays King Louis XV. In addition to bringing Depp back to a big-budget film, this part puts him in a historical setting that enables him to play nuanced, multidimensional characters in a period piece, a genre he hasn't often worked in.

Depp's drive for both familiarity and development is demonstrated by his choice to pursue both iconic and novel possibilities. He is committed to finding a balance between his continued pursuit of artistic fulfillment and his legacy as a cherished celebrity as he goes forward.

A Durable Effect

Rebuilding his career is only one aspect of Johnny Depp's new chapter; another is making a lasting impression. Depp is creating a legacy that is considerably more intricate and varied than the one that was previously characterized by tabloid scandals and courtroom dramas because of his work in both independent and major motion picture ventures, his continuous artistic reinvention, and his dedication to personal development.

Depp's latest chapter is essentially a final reclamation of his story. It's a chance for him to share his own experience, not just through the parts he plays but also through the methods he lives and works. Depp is reminding the public that he is much more than the scandals that once characterized him as he enters this next stage. His new chapter is only getting started, but he is a gifted, ambitious, and resilient artist with much more to offer.

CHAPTER 8: THE LEGACY OF JOHNNY DEPP

CULTURAL IMPACT

There is no denying Johnny Depp's influence on culture. Beyond being a Hollywood A-lister and a box office attraction, Depp has made a name for himself in popular culture thanks to his varied parts, unorthodox demeanor, and capacity to go beyond the parameters of conventional celebrity. Generations of fans have been impacted by his work on and off screen, which has also influenced public opinion and even changed our perception of celebrity culture in general. Beyond his performances, Depp has a significant cultural impact on fashion, music, the arts, and even the definition of famous.

A New Hero Type

Depp's ability to defy the stereotype of the stereotypical Hollywood leading man propelled his ascent to popularity. He adopted a more nuanced, quirky approach to his parts rather than following the traditional route of the "heartthrob" actor. His depictions of characters who were frequently misfits, rebels, or outcasts—like Willy Wonka, Edward Scissorhands, and Captain Jack Sparrow—challenged conventional notions of beauty and heroism in film. Because of their imperfections, peculiarities, and a strong sense of personality, these characters—far from being the idealized or flawless protagonists commonly found in popular movies—resonated with viewers.

Depp consequently rose to prominence as a cultural icon who embraced complexity and imperfection. His characters frequently exemplified the notion that being unique or unorthodox was not only acceptable but also deserving of praise. Younger generations, particularly those who had long felt alienated by the conventional representations of success and beauty that dominated Hollywood, found great resonance in this change in the definition of heroism and beauty in movies.

This change in how heroes are portrayed was perfectly captured by Depp's performance in *Pirates of the Caribbean* (2003). Depp portrayed Captain Jack Sparrow, an antihero who was neither completely good nor completely wicked. Despite having many flaws, his personality was endearing and incredibly unexpected. Jack Sparrow became one of the most recognizable characters in movie history thanks to this combination of qualities. With his odd demeanor and irreverent sense of humor, Depp's portrayal of Jack revolutionized the pirate genre and made him a representation of eccentric rebellion. The character swiftly established itself as a cultural icon, impacting language, fashion, and pop culture in general.

A Style Star

Johnny Depp's influence on culture has also been greatly influenced by his style. His personal style choices, which were frequently characterized by rock-and-roll edge, bohemian inspirations, and an unrepentant disdain for traditional fashion conventions, contributed to the redefining of masculinity in Hollywood. With his long hair, layered outfits, and trademark accessories (such as bracelets, rings, and scarves), Depp's gritty, unkempt look became instantly identifiable. It was a look that combined youthful rebellion with a timeless charm that conveyed both carelessness and sophistication.

This casual attitude to fashion, which conflated luxury with thrift-store style, changed the way that males, in particular, could be portrayed in the media. Young admirers responded well to Depp's appearance, and the general public soon followed suit. Numerous copycats took up Depp's distinctive look in the years after his ascent to stardom. Instead of following trends, he established his own and inspired followers to value uniqueness and genuineness, which helped him become a fashion star. His sense of style was more than just his attire; it was a manifestation of his character and creative instincts, appealing to many who disapproved of the slick, manufactured looks of popular Hollywood.

Arts and Music

Johnny Depp has always had a strong affinity for music and the arts in addition to his career as an actor. His reputation as a cultural icon has been further cemented by his passion for rock and roll and his friendships with some of the most significant artists in the world. Depp frequently works with musicians; his most famous collaboration was with rock legend Keith Richards, whose character greatly impacted Depp's portrayal of Jack Sparrow. Depp is not only involved in music because of his acting duties; he is also a musician.

Depp has played guitar in a number of ensembles, notably **P,** a collaboration with actor and musician Bill Carter, who is a close friend. In addition, Depp has worked with artists such as Marilyn Manson, Aerosmith, and even the renowned rock band The Hollywood Vampires, which he co-founded. His commitment to music demonstrates his wide range of artistic pursuits and his wish to use more than just acting to further the cultural conversation.

His artistic decisions in movies are also influenced by his love of music. Depp's love of music informs his portrayal of characters in several of his films, which feature musical elements. For instance, his performance in **The Ninth Gate (1999)** included a hauntingly evocative soundtrack, while Depp's singing prowess was on display in the darkly gorgeous musical **Sweeney Todd: The Demon Barber of Fleet Street (2007).**

Celebrity Culture Impact

Depp has had a significant and varied impact on celebrity culture. He is a unique personality in Hollywood because of his ability to preserve his seclusion and mystique in the era of social media. Depp has sought to keep his personal life as hidden from the public as possible and has refrained from interacting with the media as much as many of his contemporaries. His attraction has only grown as a result of his unwillingness to join the celebrity circus and his avoidance of the "red carpet" mentality. Depp is one of the rare celebrities who has maintained their relevance without conforming to the conventional norms of celebrity conduct because of his defiant attitude toward the accouterments of fame.

In many respects, Depp has come to represent what some refer to as "old Hollywood"—a period when celebrities were more mysterious and less approachable. His choice to disassociate himself from the intrusive nature of celebrity culture, whether through declining interviews or avoiding the spotlight, has led many to consider him a holdover from a time when genius and artistry were valued more highly than social media presence and influencer culture.

Simultaneously, Depp's turbulent personal life and widely reported legal disputes gave rise to another facet of celebrity culture: the public's ravenous appetite for drama. In contemporary celebrity culture, his legal battles with Amber Heard, the defamation trial, and the media circus that surrounded those incidents were among the most talked-about occurrences. Depp's capacity to overcome these conflicts, keep a devoted following, and regain his professional path, however, illustrates the nuanced interaction between celebrities and the media. It emphasized the potential for an artist to remake themselves in the public spotlight while highlighting the perils and strengths of celebrity.

The Jack Sparrow Global Phenomenon

As Captain Jack Sparrow in the *Pirates of the Caribbean* franchise, Johnny Depp's cultural impact has arguably been solidified more than any other single role. The character is a timeless worldwide sensation in addition to being a cherished character in movies. Jack Sparrow quickly became a cultural figure thanks to his eccentric antics, unique voice, and iconic appearance, which included dreadlocked hair, eyeliner, and tattered clothes. Audiences throughout the world were enthralled by his unorthodox brand of heroics and his ability to combine mayhem and charm.

Captain Jack Sparrow's influence goes beyond the *Pirates* movies. The figure has made appearances in video games, theme parks, products, and even in everyday speech, with expressions like "But why is the rum gone?" becoming instantly identifiable. From Halloween costumes to how swashbucklers are portrayed in subsequent movies, Depp's portrayal of Jack Sparrow has had a long-lasting effect on how pirates are portrayed in popular culture.

In addition to transforming the pirate genre with Jack Sparrow, Depp cemented his status as one of the most inventive, surprising, and significant performers of his generation.

Final Thought: A Durable Impact

Since his distinct fusion of artistry, rebellion, and mystique has struck a chord with people worldwide, Johnny Depp's cultural influence is indisputable. Depp has left a lasting legacy that goes beyond the screen, from his unorthodox attitude to fashion and celebrity to his impact on how heroes are portrayed in movies. His ability to reinvent himself both personally and professionally has cemented his place in cultural history as one of the most influential and enduring figures in contemporary entertainment, and his work continues to inspire new generations of performers, directors, and fans. Johnny Depp continues to be a genuine cultural figure, whether it is because of his famous roles, his dedication to artistic expression, or his impact on how we view celebrity and uniqueness.

ENDURING FANDOM

Johnny Depp's devoted following is evidence of the strong bond he has built with viewers over the years. In addition to winning over millions of fans, his distinct fusion of skill, quirkiness, and genuineness has solidified his place as one of the most adored performers of his generation. Depp's supporters have remained steadfastly devoted despite the scandals, personal hardships, and turbulent years that have periodically jeopardized his career. This has resulted in a phenomenon that goes beyond conventional fandom and is firmly anchored in identification, emotion, and a common passion.

The Depp Fanbase's Loyalty

Since the beginning of his career, Johnny Depp has drawn a wide range of admirers who value his roles as well as the uniqueness and sincerity he brought to each character. This commitment to the man, the character he has developed, and the way he has remained true to himself in a society that frequently demands conformity goes beyond simple appreciation for his acting prowess. Fans of Depp actively participate in his work journey rather than merely watching it from a distance. They applaud his creative choices, his unorthodox ones, and the audacious way he still defies Hollywood conventions.

The age range and worldwide reach of Depp's fandom are among its most remarkable features. Depp has continued to appeal to a wide range of audiences, from young teens who first saw his work through the **Pirates of the Caribbean** films to older generations who grew up with his more independent parts in movies like **Edward Scissorhands** and **What's Eating Gilbert Grape.** Fans from many walks of life can identify with the characters he portrays because of his wide range of roles, which speak to various cultural contexts and experiences.

Depp's ability to establish a deeper connection with his fans is what has sustained their loyalty even during his most trying public moments. Fans have been able to relate to Depp on a personal level because of his sensitivity as an actor and public figure. His openness to sharing his feelings, whether through his roles or personal experiences, speaks to those who have frequently felt excluded or misunderstood. Fans of Depp frequently relate to his outsider status; they regard Depp as a defender of individualism and, like his characters, have accepted their differences.

The Effect of Jack Sparrow

Johnny Depp's portrayal of Captain Jack Sparrow in **Pirates of the Caribbean** was without a doubt the part that cemented his status as a pop cultural legend and strengthened his bond with his followers. In addition to being a financial success, Jack Sparrow grew to represent Depp's style of acting and originality. Jack Sparrow became instantly recognizable—so much so that it transcended the film and took on a life of its own in the cultural zeitgeist—and the film series became a huge worldwide hit.

Jack Sparrow was portrayed by Depp in a way that was unique among pirates in movie history. He was portrayed with a sense of disarray, a mischievous rebelliousness, and an idiosyncratic appeal that went against the conventional heroic ideal. Depp's admirers were drawn to Jack Sparrow because of his eccentricity, uniqueness, and unpredictable nature. Fans learned to value these attributes, and many of them incorporated Jack's swagger and quips into their idioms. Jack Sparrow became a lasting presence in popular culture because of his distinctive demeanor, which included his recognizable gait, his slurred speech, and his nuanced moral compass.

It is impossible to overestimate Jack Sparrow's influence on Depp's fandom. Depp's portrayal of the pirate served as a springboard for many admirers to appreciate his work on a deeper level. A whole new generation of fans was introduced to Depp through the **Pirates** franchise, and they were enthralled not only by the spectacle and adventure but also by the nuance and complexity of his portrayal. Fan conferences, fan literature, paraphernalia, and innumerable internet forums devoted to Jack Sparrow and Depp himself were all products of the fandom around the character. Such intense loyalty is uncommon for a character, and the everlasting affection for Jack Sparrow is evidence of the long-lasting influence of Depp's artistic brilliance.

The Influence of Online Communities and Social Media

Fans of Depp have discovered new ways to show their love and support in the era of social media. Fans of Depp may now express their affection for the actor, talk about his work, and offer assistance during trying times on sites like Twitter, Instagram, TikTok, and fan forums. During his judicial fights, hashtags like #JusticeForJohnnyDepp gained popularity, fostering a sense of unity among supporters who were outspoken about their belief in his innocence. This online movement showed how social media can bring people together from all over the world and foster an active online community that followed the actor's path, especially when Depp was under public criticism.

As a way to keep celebrating Depp's work, his followers have also embraced the internet sphere. Online platforms are overflowing with fan art, tributes, movies, and memes dedicated to his characters, demonstrating the fanbase's inventiveness and passion. Despite the highs and lows of his professional career, Depp's reputation has endured thanks to his unwavering presence in the digital realm. By continuing to promote his art and support him in ways that go beyond conventional advertising campaigns, his supporters actively contribute to the development of his public persona.

Depp's admirers have developed their unique groups and subcultures via these online platforms. Fan conventions, like the one for **Pirates of the Caribbean**, have grown in popularity as yearly occasions for fans to get together and celebrate their favorite movies and characters. Fans can meet their idol, share their enthusiasm with others, and lose themselves in a universe centered around Depp's characters at these gatherings. To provide fans with a closer connection to the world of Johnny Depp, several of these events include cosplay contests, fan panels, and exclusive Q&A sessions with the actor's colleagues.

Fandom's Contribution to Depp's Career Comeback

After years of personal and professional upheaval, Depp's career has rebounded in large part due to the steadfast devotion of his fan base. Many in the industry questioned whether Depp would ever regain his former prominence after his legal disputes and controversies put his career on hiatus. But a major factor in his comeback to fame was the strength of his fan base. Depp's supporters made sure his voice was heard in the media and helped change the public perception through their internet campaigns, petitions, and outspoken support.

Despite years of unfavorable publicity, Depp's recent films, like **Minamata (2020)**, proved that there was still a market for his work. His admirers, who had stood by him through his worst moments, were prepared to welcome him back on TV. Depp's comeback demonstrates the impact that a long-lasting fandom can have on an actor's career and demonstrates how important ardent fans' support can be for an artist to overcome hardship.

A Connection For Life

For many of Johnny Depp's most devoted followers, their love for him has grown beyond simple devotion and has established a lasting bond. Over the years, Depp's fan base has remained active due to his capacity to change and take on new challenges on both a personal and professional level. Even though Depp has had his share of public scandals, his supporters have supported him because they see him as more than just a famous person navigating the challenges of public life.

The longevity of Depp's fan base further demonstrates how timeless his work is. From the iconic Captain Jack Sparrow to the misunderstood Edward Scissorhands, his roles have woven themselves into the fabric of culture. Generations after generation watch, discuss and enjoy his flicks. The foundation of support Depp's fans have constructed for him is unchanging, and as long as he keeps creating, his devoted following will be there to celebrate his next phase of success.

Ultimately, Johnny Depp's enduring cultural relevance is demonstrated by his fan base, which is more than just a reflection of his work. Depp's followers have contributed to the legacy of one of the most recognizable performers of our time by their steadfast devotion, artistic expression, and active participation.

A LEGEND BEYOND TIME

Johnny Depp's career is timeless, elevating him from a Hollywood actor to a cultural and cinematic icon whose influence endured for centuries. Throughout his remarkable career, Depp has not only created a wide range of memorable characters, but he has also shaped the entire definition of what it means to be a worldwide celebrity. His desire to defy expectations, push limits, and stay resolutely true to his creative vision is the foundation of his influence on the film business, pop culture, and the artistic community, which goes well beyond his performances. In addition to his extraordinary talent, Depp is a legend for his ability to stay inspirational and relevant in a world that is changing all the time.

His Characters' Timeless Appeal

Being able to play characters who are both timeless and current is one of Johnny Depp's most notable career traits. Depp's roles have never been limited to a particular period or genre, from his breakthrough performance in **Edward Scissorhands (1990)** to his legendary portrayal of Captain Jack Sparrow in the *Pirates of the Caribbean* series. His characters are beautiful because they are global and unaffected by the historical or cultural settings of the movies in which they are featured. Instead, they capture fundamental human feelings like isolation, longing, resistance, and rebellion that audiences everywhere can relate to.

Consider his performance as Edward Scissorhands. A misunderstood, kind soul with scissorblades for hands, the caricature quickly came to represent the outsider. People from all walks of life found great resonance in Edward's emotional complexity and his quest for belonging. Even though **Edward Scissorhands** was a movie of its day, its themes of acceptance and self-identity are timeless, allowing new generations to rediscover the character as they struggle with similar challenges of conformity and alienation. Like Depp's other well-known characters, Edward's popularity cuts beyond the constraints of the film's production period, demonstrating Depp's talent for creating characters that appeal to audiences of all ages.

Similar to this, Captain Jack Sparrow has gained such cultural relevance that it is hard to picture contemporary film without him thanks to his distinct combination of charm, irreverence, and vulnerability. Jack Sparrow, a character who chooses freedom and adventure over the norm, has come to represent anti-establishment resistance. His popularity extends well beyond the **Pirates of the Caribbean** film series; he has impacted pop culture's depiction of pirates as well as language and attire. His ability to create a character that feels ageless and endlessly relevant is demonstrated by Depp's depiction of Jack, which has cemented the character as one of the most adored icons in movie history.

A Time-Defying Artist

Johnny Depp is an artist in the purest sense of the word, not just an actor. He has always approached his work with a strong dedication to honesty, frequently taking risks that defy the expectations of traditional Hollywood acting. Depp has distinguished himself as a genuine trailblazer in the industry by accepting parts that are quirky, unconventional, and occasionally downright strange. Depp has chosen a career path characterized by artistic integrity, working with visionary directors like Tim Burton, Terry Gilliam, and Jim Jarmusch to create films that are as much about creativity and expression as they are about entertainment. This is in contrast to many actors who choose roles that ensure commercial success.

Depp's unafraid acting style has enabled him to sustain a dynamic career that deviates from the usual paths taken by Hollywood celebrities. Depp's decisions are always driven by the desire to delve into uncharted areas of both himself and his profession, whether he's portraying a paranoid journalist in **Fear and Loathing in Las Vegas (1998),** a reclusive chocolatier in **Charlie and the Chocolate Factory (2005),** or a legendary gangster in **Public Enemies (2009).** A defining characteristic of Depp's career has been his inability to fit into preconceived notions and be typecast. His dedication to originality and genuineness is what has made him a timeless character in a field that is undergoing constant change.

A Generation-Span Influence

The impact that Johnny Depp has had on subsequent generations of actors, directors, and artists is not limited to his work. His embrace of the ridiculous, the fantastical, and the profoundly human in ways that challenge both audiences and other artists has made him a touchstone for those who want to push the limits of traditional narrative. A new generation of talent has been influenced by Depp's legacy as an actor, viewing him not only as a celebrity but also as a symbol of what can be achieved when one is not afraid to take chances and pursue their creative goals.

Depp's impact is also felt on a larger cultural scale. His performances, particularly in movies like **Edward Scissorhands** and **Pirates of the Caribbean**, have shaped our perception of the actor's place in society. Depp's characters frequently exhibit a certain liberation from the limitations of conventional heroics, which helps them connect with viewers who are increasingly turning away from flat characters in favor of ones with more nuance and complexity. The popularity of antiheroes and ethically dubious characters in modern films can be partly ascribed to Depp's performances. In this sense, Depp helped redefine what a **"hero"** is in contemporary popular culture in addition to bringing about a change in cinematic storytelling.

The Signature of Classic Style

In addition to his acting career, Depp's style has had a lasting impact on celebrity culture and fashion. He has become a style icon in his right thanks to his distinctive bohemian, eclectic, and carefree look. Depp's sense of originality and genuineness, which are qualities that are entirely consistent with his public character, determine his style rather than current trends. Depp's style has stayed constant over the years, reflecting the same rebellious spirit that defines his on-screen personas, whether he's wearing a fitted suit on the red carpet or a more laid-back, rustic appearance.

Numerous admirers have been encouraged to embrace their originality and reject traditional fashion standards in favor of personal expression by their distinctive sense of style. Depp's style, which frequently combines gypsy, vintage Americana, and rock & roll components, has produced a timeless look that transcends simple apparel. His nonconformity is reflected in this attitude, which both fashionistas and fans have embraced.

A Permanent Influence on Popular Culture

Johnny Depp's cultural influence is ingrained in pop culture and extends well beyond his movie roles and wardrobe choices. Depp has had a significant impact on music, literature, art, and even social movements through the characters he has developed and the public image he has fostered. He has been able to rise above the Hollywood bubble because of his partnerships with musicians, involvement in charitable endeavors, and ties to the fine art world. Through his artistic endeavors outside of acting, Depp has been able to build a rich and diverse legacy that reflects his unwavering quest for artistic expression.

Furthermore, Depp's continued cultural significance has been facilitated by his capacity to interact with fans both in person and virtually. His unique position in the public consciousness is demonstrated by the steadfast devotion of his fan following, which has endured despite both personal and professional setbacks. His admirers actively participate in the continuing conversation about his life and career rather than merely viewing his work. Mutual respect, admiration, and a shared enthusiasm characterize Depp's relationship with his fans, which has only grown stronger over time.

An Enduring Legacy

Long after the credits have rolled on Johnny Depp's last movie, his legacy will live on. Depp has solidified his status as a star in the entertainment world with his memorable parts, his bold acting technique, his style, and his close bond with his followers. His impact on fashion, society, and film is indisputable, and his ability to stay relevant across generations guarantees that his influence will last for a very long time. In addition to being a great actor, Johnny Depp is a cultural influence whose contributions to society and the arts will continue to influence the globe for a very long time. He is a timeless legend whose legacy will endure forever.

CONCLUSION

One cannot help but be amazed by the intricacy of the guy who has enthralled the world time and time again as the last scene of Johnny Depp's extraordinary life tale plays out. His trip, which has included high adventure, surprising turns, and poignant moments of vulnerability, has been nothing short of cinematic. It is evident to those who have closely watched Depp's career that his life is everything but a straightforward story of success and wealth. It's a tale of successes and failures, artistic experimentation and public criticism, self-reinvention, and lasting legacy. Depp is a contradictory character, much like the parts he has played so frequently, and this exploration of his life has pulled back the curtain to show the man behind the headlines.

One fact, however, emerges as we complete this chapter in Depp's life: his artistic talent endures forever. Despite the upheaval, difficulties, and controversies, Johnny Depp's legacy as a famous performer is cemented—not just because of the roles he played or the movies he starred in, but also because of the lasting impression he had on the foundation of contemporary entertainment. It is impossible to overestimate his impact on society, cinema, and even how we see celebrity and individual identity. Depp's ability to change and give life to the most outrageous and fearless personas stoked a passion in the hearts of fans all over the world from the first time he appeared on screen.

His narrative is far from over, though. Like any great artist, Depp is still a work in progress, a changing person whose path is determined by his constant self-reinvention rather than the parts he has performed. The world saw him struggle personally, withstand adversity, and come out stronger in the end; his legacy was molded by the strength with which he addressed his obstacles rather than by the difficulties themselves. He continues to rethink what it means to be an artist in a society that frequently demands perfection, and his tale is not one of failure but one of perseverance.

As we consider his legacy, we are reminded that, like the best gripping tales, Johnny Depp's life is about how it keeps going rather than about coming to an end. He is now more than just an actor; he represents the artist's battle to remain unique in the face of excessive demands. His influence extends beyond the screen and permeates the lives of people who dare to pursue their own goals at whatever cost. Ultimately, Johnny Depp's journey serves as a reminder that genuine artistry is about having the guts to stay true to oneself and the work, not just about the parts one plays or the recognition one gets.

As this biography draws to a close, we are therefore at the beginning of the next chapter rather than its conclusion. The tale of Johnny Depp, full of creativity, adversity, and success, is far from over. This is only one more step in a journey that will continue to develop and leave us in the wonder of the mysterious, fearless, and enduring force that is Johnny Depp, according to the world that has been enthralled by his every move.

Made in United States
Cleveland, OH
28 June 2025

18102459R00085